Teaching Primaries

Teaching Primaries

Ruth Beechick

ACCENT BOOKS

Denver, Colorado

ACCENT BOOKS
A division of Accent Publications, Inc.
12100 W. Sixth Avenue
P.O. Box 15337
Denver, Colorado 80215

Copyright © 1980 Accent Publications, Inc.
Printed in the United States of America

Library of Congress Catalog Card Number: 80-66723

ISBN 0-89636-054-7

CONTENTS

Preface

In this book I have tried to give a practical mix of theory and how-to. I think teachers want enough information on theory that they can make up their own minds about it, but they don't usually want it in the depth that researchers or curriculum planners require. This book tries to hit that happy medium. It also tries to show what theory means when translated into the classroom. For instance, it doesn't merely tell you that your teaching should be on a concrete level, but it gives some insight into what that means, and some suggestions for how to do it.

This book focuses at times on Sunday school teaching but it does consider the primary child and his Christian growth in a general way. So teachers in other Christian ministries should find help here, too.

When I use the term "Christian education" in this book, I mean, specifically, the child's education into Christianity, and I take the position that the Bible is the center of such education. In a larger sense Christian education can refer to all of a person's education from a Christian or Biblical perspective, and I believe such education is needed. But this book is not that wide in scope. It should find its best use in church-related ministries with primary children, and with students who are preparing for such ministries.

I wish to thank the many teachers who have written to me and talked to me about their problems and needs in teaching. And I thank those who graciously let me visit their classrooms. It is due largely to all of you that this is not an "ivory tower" sort of book, but has much of the classroom in it. And, of course, I cannot overlook the contribution of the hundreds of delightful children who put up with me as their teacher and who cooperated in my researches. It is my joy to share with you readers what they have taught me.

Ruth Beechick

1 Meet the Primary Child

- *Physical Development*
- *Social-Emotional Development*
- *Development of Moral Reasoning*
- *Spiritual Development*

"Jewoosalem," said Lisa. Then she realized that didn't sound right so she tried again. "Jewoosalem."

"It's hard to say Jerusalem when your two front teeth are missing," said the teacher.

"I just lost another tooth," said Lisa, brightly. "See?"

"How did you do that?" asked Mrs. Miller, walking closer.

"I wiggled it and pulled it out."

"You did! When?"

"While you were telling the story."

"Oh, you were brave. Some people panic when they're going to lose a tooth. But you just took it out and listened to the story."

Lisa and her peers are competent little people in many ways. Teachers of primaries have a joyful task working with them and getting to know them. In this chapter we will look at some other physical characteristics these children have in common besides losing teeth. After a section on physical development, we will look at social-emotional, moral, and spiritual development. Major views of mental development are reserved for Chapter 2.

Physical Development

The rapid growth of preschool years slows down during the primary years. The younger primary child does not have a great deal of strength, and he tires easily in activities which require the use of his strength. Older primary boys have a rapid increase in strength so that their strength doubles. This usually happens during third grade and on into fourth grade. From this time on, boys are stronger than girls.

Generally speaking, then, boys and girls can participate together in the same physical activities during first and second grades. But during third grade, boys' activity tends to become rougher, and the girls begin to separate themselves from it. A wise teacher will allow the boys their rougher play and will not try to keep all activity at the girls' level.

The energy of primary children continues at a high level through these years. It is not normal for primary children to sit still, as adults, for long periods of time. Classroom schedules and learning activities must always be planned with this characteristic in mind. Let the children learn a verse through physical activities, instead of through watching. (See Chapter 4.) Let the children walk about the room to get their readers or crayons or other supplies, instead of sitting still while you hand out all the supplies. Include in your lesson plan some movement activities. Be soldiers marching around Jericho or be farmers sowing wheat. A liberal sprinkling of physical activity in your class period will enable your children to sit still for times of listening. And the activities themselves can be learning too, so your children profit doubly from this arrangement.

Coordination is much improved over the preschool years, so the primary child makes great strides in complex motor skills. He learns to jump rope, skate, swim. He is better at using pencils and crayons.

The primary years could be known as the most restless period of life because of the increased coordination along with purposeless energy. In other words, the primary child can now do things better and has plenty of energy with which to do them, but he generally lacks purpose for all this activity. The trick for the teacher is to use this coordination and skill and energy, instead of repressing them. Add purpose to the energy. Help the child achieve learning through it.

Ability to sing on tune is developed in the children who did not already develop it in the preschool years.

The ability to speak new languages without accent is beginning to be lost. Very young children can make the sounds in any language, so they learn to use those sounds in whatever language or languages they are exposed to. Other sounds are extinguished from their repertoires by about age 7.

This means that a person learning a new language after about 7 cannot speak it as a native of that language. But children who are bilingual or multilingual in their early years retain ability to make more speech sounds. So they will have better ability to speak languages in later years.

Social-Emotional Development

The school-age child is developing greater emotional stability through give and take with other children. The child has a strong desire to be a member of groups, and teachers can use this motivation to teach children better social behavior.

Primaries need much guidance in how to behave with others. Often their teasings and aggressions are simply clumsy attempts at friendliness. Children want others to respond to them and sometimes they go about it in aggressive ways. When their efforts bring forth anger in others they may be bewildered.

Here, more than anywhere else, you will want to be a guide and not an authoritarian figure. When a child says, "Teacher, he hit me," the quick and easy response may be to make a decision about which child is in the wrong and then reprimand or punish him. But this helps neither child toward better social skills, and it puts you in the trap of having to act as referee in countless childish squabbles. That can drain your energy and time from more profitable teaching.

It is better to help the complaining child find his own way to handle the problem. Help him see some of his options. You might just say, "Well, do you want to sit by someone else?" Surprisingly, children will not always take the option to move. Sometimes the child has chosen to sit by the friend who hit him. He may even have provoked the tiff, and then tried to get you on his side. When you fail to take sides the children work it out themselves and move one step closer to social maturity.

Primaries can learn to be sympathetic toward others. They can sympathize with a bully for his unhappiness. They can learn not to react with anger but to return good for evil. They can do something kind for a child who is handicapped, or shy, or slower to learn. This doesn't mean they will always do it. But primary group life with all its frictions is a good laboratory for learning these skills and attitudes.

When one child is usually the center of trouble, you can give extra help to him. Show him better ways to act, and help him see the rewards of acting in these ways. Help him see that the children like him better and that he is happier when he does good.

In matters of behavior, you have basically two main approaches. You can be authoritarian and impose your rules on the children while you are in charge. Or you can take the teaching approach and guide the children toward better self-discipline. This will go with them even when you are not around. You may develop your own private mixture of these two approaches, teaching when you can, and being authoritarian at times when the teaching approach is working too slowly and vigorous primary behavior is interfering with other important matters. This mixture is probably what most teachers with a commonsense approach to teaching will choose.

Development of Moral Reasoning

In our day, one hardly speaks of moral development without mentioning the name Kohlberg. Lawrence Kohlberg has identified Piaget-style "stages" and levels in moral reasoning. Here is a brief description of the four levels and the stages included in each.

Premoral Level. Stage 0: The infant and toddler cannot be said to understand or reason at all about moral issues. He has no conception of an obligation to others or to authority. For him, good is what is pleasant, and bad is what is painful. He does what he can do or wants to do.

Preconventional Level. The child who is disciplined grows to respond to the way his society labels good and bad, or right and wrong. He responds because of consequences to himself. *Stage 1:* In this first stage the child is guided by punishment or reward. He defers to authority or power not out of respect but because avoiding punishment is a "good" in itself. *Stage 2:* In this stage the child is guided by personal satisfaction and occasionally the satisfaction of others. His actions are a means of achieving satisfaction. This stage is characterized by the saying, "You be good to me and I'll be good to you." Many primary children are on Stages 1 or 2 of the Preconventional Level.

Conventional Level. At this level the person responds to society's expectations for reasons beyond himself—for loyalty. A few primary children reach Stage 3 or 4 in the Conventional Level, although the "normal" age for this is about thirteen. A good many adults never grow beyond this level. *Stage 3:* At this stage the person is guided by the expectations of others. He acts for the approval of others. An older term for this stage might be the "other-directed" person. Kohlberg calls it the "good-boy" stage. *Stage 4:* At this stage the person understands something of the need for authority, rules, and social order. Respect for these is a "good." Duty is a "good."

Principled Level. At the principled level a person tries to find values that have justification in their own right, apart from any supporting person or group. This level is reached, if at all, by late adolescence or the early twenties. Kohlberg thinks his evidence shows that if a person does not reach this principled level by these "normal" ages, he is thwarted in his development and will never attain this level. *Stage 5:* This is somewhat like the social-contract idea. The standards of Stage 5 reasoning tend to be the standards that have been evaluated and agreed upon by the whole society. But there is openness to changing the law when that seems best. *Stage 6:* Standards are now in the individual conscience rather than in laws or social agreements. Principles are self-chosen on the basis of universality and logical consistency. These principles are abstractions and are not concrete rules found in religions or philosophies or elsewhere. Kohlberg believes the highest of these abstractions is justice. He has largely dropped Stage 6 from his research because, he says, so few people attain this stage.

A Christian looking at Kohlberg's research will have some questions, among them being the finding of justice as the highest principle. One wonders if the research were done among Christians only, whether another principle, such as the "love of Christ," might be on top.

The love of Christ motivated Paul. Jesus said that on love hangs all the law. Paul observes that the law is a schoolmaster to bring us to Christ. So it is a Scriptural teaching that law comes first. Law leads to Christ and to love. In a sense this is what Kohlberg has found in his research. The earlier law levels of moral reasoning are a necessary foundation to the higher principled level.

The Christian teacher needs to put God into all teaching on moral reasoning. At Stage 1 where the child is guided by punishment and reward consequences, it is entirely appropriate to teach that God punishes evil and rewards good. Many Bible stories show this clearly and concretely. In present day life God may not punish as swiftly as in the Ananias and Sapphira story, but more delayed as in the flood story. But swift or delayed, it still is a truth that God punishes sin. This is a reason for choosing right. For children at Stage 1 it can be important. Along with the fact that parent or teacher punishes, God punishes too. This lines up all authority in the child's life on the side of "good."

As the Stage 1 child does good in order to avoid punishment, he occasionally experiences the satisfaction of being good. This moves him to Stage 2. He comes to understand that doing something good for another brings him the satisfaction of having a friend or the pleasure of working or playing together with another. These satisfactions he can see as reasons for being good at Stage 2.

As the child sees satisfactions in being good to others, he can be led into Stage 3. The approval of teacher and peers becomes important. Put God in here, too. Teach the children that God is pleased when they do good. The child learns what that means by seeing approval in you or his parents or his peers.

Of course this brings up the theological argument that our righteousnesses are as filthy rags in God's sight, and that we need Christ's righteousness in order to please God. Some would prefer to teach the children that they cannot please God while they are not saved. The other side of this coin is that children must learn God's law of right and wrong so they can see the need of a Savior. The schoolmaster idea again—the law brings us to Christ.

No "commonsense" teacher is going to let meanness reign in the classroom while she shrugs and says, "These children can't be good until they find Christ's righteousness." Surely every teacher works out his or her own balance, somehow, of teaching about salvation, yet also teaching that God wants us to be good.

Discussion of moral dilemmas is one of the best ways to help children move up the ladder of moral reasoning. Remember, they cannot jump up this ladder, but only move up one step at a time. If you try to talk about abstract principles, such as justice or love, to your Stage 1 children they will not understand at all. But reasoning one or two steps above them on the ladder sounds good to them, and opens up new thought, even though they may not yet take that as their own reasoning.

For instance, you may discuss the story of Isaac and the wells. Should Isaac have fought to use his wells? After all, he dug them; they were his. Is it right to just give up a well, and move on and dig another? Stage 1 or 2 children will not understand a reasoning about "rights" versus a "turn the other cheek" philosophy. These abstractions are beyond them. But they will appreciate a Stage 3 answer, that God was pleased. In the story God appeared and showed His approval. Children at Stages 1 and 2 can somehow sense that Stage 3 reasoning is better than a Stage 1 (God might punish him if he fights). And exposure in discussions to such reasoning, just a little above their own, will help lead children to higher levels themselves.

Incidentally, when this story is translated into a line at the drinking fountain, and what a child should do when another pushes in front of him, some primary children can see the Stage 3 reasoning and some can actually act on it.

As another example, you might discuss Abraham's rescue of Lot. It is too abstract and "principled" to talk about the morality of war—whether it is right or wrong, when it is right or wrong, and so forth. But the Stage 3 reasoning of loyalty to family, of being the "good boy," of gaining approval by God, all are understandable.

It is important to notice that all such teaching concerns moral *reasoning*, not moral *acting*. And knowing what is right does not insure doing what is right. Kohlberg's research shows that people at the principled level are more likely to do what they believe is right, than those at lower levels. Thus the interest these days in pushing more people up to the top of the ladder.

The Christian should be more concerned that God is at every level. The Preconventional child needs guidance by godly parents and teachers. The values he appropriates from them can later become his own. The Conventional Level child who understands approval and rules and law should be guided by God's law and God's approval. Since many people live the rest of their lives at these law stages, it wouldn't be too bad for society if they all had a firm grounding in God's law.

Teaching on the Principled Level is not generally appropriate at primary ages.

Spiritual Development

Of course no teacher thinks of a child in terms of his physical self, his mental self, his spiritual self, and so on. The child is seen in a more wholistic way. It is only in books like this that he gets so split up. Even when teachers do split off the spiritual and say, "Please pray that Donnie will be saved," it may be because Donnie is a behavior problem and she is hoping a spiritual birth will solve some of the child's problems.

And well it may. The spiritual affects the total self, just as any other aspect does.

And if we are going to separate any one part of the child for special attention it ought to be the spiritual. The Bible speaks rather plainly of the spiritual life that is in some people but not in others. It is clear that this spiritual life must be "born," and that it should grow, and that it will never die. What could be of greater concern to a teacher than this eternal life? Long after the child's reading problems are solved, his social life is smoothed out, and his great energy has simmered down, his spiritual life abides. In this life and the next.

This is why most teachers struggle with the reading problems, the behavior problems, and the wiggling, noisy bodies. They know the eternal worth of the work they are doing.

And primary teachers have the privilege of being where most of the "births" can happen. With good teaching, the general pattern is that a few children are saved at preschool ages, most of the rest during primary years, and a few in the junior years. One thing this means for primary teachers is that they should be prepared to teach salvation and to lead children to Christ. This matter is treated more fully in Chapter 3.

This should have meaning, also, for evangelistic outreaches such as Vacation Bible School and bus ministries. If the greatest potential for salvation is at school age instead of preschool, and if staff and resources are limited, then those resources should perhaps be spent where they will do the most good—with school-age children. Of course, a church may choose to minister to preschoolers as a way to reach parents, or some other reason, but it is better, then, to see clearly that evangelism (of the children) is not the main goal.

After salvation, comes growth. Here, the teaching a child receives is extremely important. As most of these young children do not read the Bible for themselves, they must learn from their teachers, which ideally should include parents. Week by week you will teach the children some of the most important things they will ever learn. What is God like? Who is Jesus? How do we worship God? How do we talk to Him? Who is the Holy Spirit? All the important themes of Scripture can be opened up to the primary child. And he will grow through the Word.

In Christian education there is a need to define Christian growth more specifically—to break it down into smaller parts. This will help curriculum planners and teachers in evaluating and in setting appropriate goals. We present here a list in the form of developmental tasks. The lists for all ages are given, so that you can see what comes before primary and what comes after. And you can see how the primary tasks (included in the elementary school years) fit into the total growth pattern.

Spiritual Developmental Tasks of Preschool
  1. Experiencing love, security, discipline, joy, worship.

2. Beginning to develop awareness and concepts of God, Jesus, and other basic Christian realities.
3. Developing attitudes toward God, Jesus, church, self, Bible.
4. Beginning to develop concepts of right and wrong.

Spiritual Developmental Tasks of Elementary School Years
1. Receiving and acknowledging Jesus Christ as Savior and Lord.
2. Growing awareness of Christian love and responsibility in relationships with others.
3. Continuing to build concepts of basic Christian realities.
4. Learning basic Bible teachings adequate for personal faith and everyday Christian living, including teachings in these areas:
   a. prayer in daily life
   b. the Bible in daily life
   c. Christian friendships
   d. group worship
   e. responsibility for serving God
   f. basic knowledge of God, Jesus, Holy Spirit, creation, angelic beings, Heaven, Hell, sin, salvation, Bible literature and history
5. Developing healthy attitudes toward self.

Spiritual Developmental Tasks of Adolescence
1. Learning to show Christian love in everyday life.
2. Continuing to develop healthy attitudes toward self.
3. Developing Bible knowledge and intellectual skills adequate for meeting intellectual assaults on faith.
4. Achieving strength of Christian character adequate for meeting anti-Christian social pressures.
5. Accepting responsibility for Christian service in accordance with growing abilities.
6. Learning to make life decisions on the basis of eternal Christian values.

7. Increasing self-discipline to "seek those things which are above."

Spiritual Developmental Tasks of Maturity
1. Accepting responsibility for one's own continued growth and learning.
2. Accepting Biblical responsibilities toward God and toward others.
3. Living a unified, purposeful life centered upon God.

This list assumes a normally good Christian home and church environment. So you may have in your primary class some children without this kind of background who are "retarded" in their spiritual development. With such children you will have to work on tasks at the preschool level to bring them to readiness for the elementary level.

If a child has not experienced love in his early life he may have to experience it first with you before he can understand God's love and be brought to salvation. If a child has never heard of God or Jesus or the Bible, he will be at the preschool level in your class—beginning to develop these concepts.

In all of these tasks there is this kind of necessity for the earlier tasks to precede the later ones. Another example is that a child must experience discipline in his early years in order to develop self-discipline at later years. And discipline is a prerequisite for learning of all kinds. Still another example is that a good attitude toward self in the early years is necessary for a growing awareness of and concern for others in later years.

So one characteristic of this list is that the tasks have a logical, positive relationship across the ages. That is, the earlier tasks lead to the later. Earlier tasks are readiness for the later. Earlier tasks cannot be skipped to arrive at the later ones.

A second characteristic of the list is the logical interrelationships of tasks at any one age. For instance, at the preschool level those who hear about God and Jesus in an atmosphere of love, security, and joyfulness are the ones likely to be developing good attitudes toward them. And those who experience love and discipline are those who can develop concepts of right and wrong. At elementary level, those who are gaining the important basic Bible learnings will be increasingly aware of the need for Christian love and responsibility in their relationships with others. Put another way, if development in one area is poor for a child, his development in the other areas is likely to be poor also. And good development in one area helps along with it good development in the others. They grow together.

So these spiritual tasks can be see as 1) being interrelated at each age level, and 2) being sequentially related across the ages. This makes for what might be called an "expanded definition" of Christian growth. This definition breaks it down into smaller, more manageable pieces. With smaller pieces, you can better analyze where your children are and you can be more specific in the goals you set for your own teaching.

READING CHECK

1. It is good to let the children get up and obtain their own supplies.   T   F

2. Bilingual children have an advantage over other children in learning languages later in life.   T   F

3. When quarrels erupt it is important to figure out which child is to blame.   T   F

4. Primary children are too individualistic to work together well in groups.   T   F

5. Most primary children are at the preconventional level of moral reasoning.   T   F

6. At the preconventional level, rewards and punishment are effective motivations to good behavior.   T   F

7. When a child is saved he jumps to a higher level on Kohlberg's scale.   T   F

8. It is possible for Christians to be at various levels on Kohlberg's scale, including the low ones.   T   F

9. A list of developmental tasks shows the order of growth, meaning that the early tasks must precede the later ones. T   F

10. The quality of teaching has nothing to do with salvation since salvation is a work of the Holy Spirit.   T   F

Answers: 1—T, 2—T, 3—F, 4—F, 5—T, 6—T, 7—F, 8—T, 9—T, 10—F

2 Thinking and Learning

- *Developmental Theory*
- *Behaviorist Theory*
- *Needs Theory*
- *Concrete Thinking*
- *Poetic Thinking*

Learning psychologists have been busy in recent decades telling us all how we think. A history professor commented, "I don't think the way they think I think."

Many of us have perhaps felt like the history professor at times as we read about how people are supposed to learn and to think. At other times we may have seen a bit of ourselves in the writings and we respond, "Yes, that's just the way it happens with me."

Since we are made in the image of God, there is much more in the human mind and heart than anyone can fathom. No learning theory can say it all. Teaching cannot be reduced to a simple formula. We need to approach the study of learning with a full realization of these limitations. If we do this, we find our study helps us grow in understanding the children we work with. If we don't—if we think the theories can give us absolute laws (always start with a need, always have a behavioral objective, etc.)—then we will not profit nearly so much from them.

With this view in mind, we will look at some theories which are now given a prominent place in Christian education.

Developmental Theory

Developmental theory in our day is almost synonymous with the name Piaget, although Bruner and others have also contributed to this way of looking at the mind. This theory tries to describe for us the development of the mind. Emphasis is on the "workings" of the mind and not on the content. For instance, studies of these theorists can tell us whether children of primary age can relate two ideas and come up with a conclusion, but they tell us nothing about whether any particular ideas should be taught. This differentiation is rather important for understanding Piaget's theory, as we will see more clearly in a moment.

Piaget's now-famous "stages" in development of the mind are diagramed below. For brevity we have omitted the sensory-motor stage of the first two years and have omitted subdivisions of the stages which are shown. The child in this diagram is thinking about a well-known Piaget experiment. You have shown two identical glasses of water, and you ask, "Which glass has more water, or are they the same?" The child, seeing the water at the same height, responds that they are the same. Then you pour one glass into a tall, thin container and you pour the other into a short, fat container and ask your question again. The diagram in Figure 1 shows the results.

The first stage shown here is sometimes called the intuitive stage and sometimes called the preoperational stage. It extends roughly from age 2 to about ages 6 and 7, with variations, of course, in many children. Here the child centers on what he perceives. Most children in this experiment notice especially, or "center" on, the aspect of height and say that the tall glass has more water.

The next stage shown here is called the concrete operational stage. This extends, generally speaking, from the ages of 6/7 to 11/12, again with variations in some children. The child here no longer centers his thinking on the state of the glasses before him. He now can perform the mental operations of reversing the action. He can reason that since

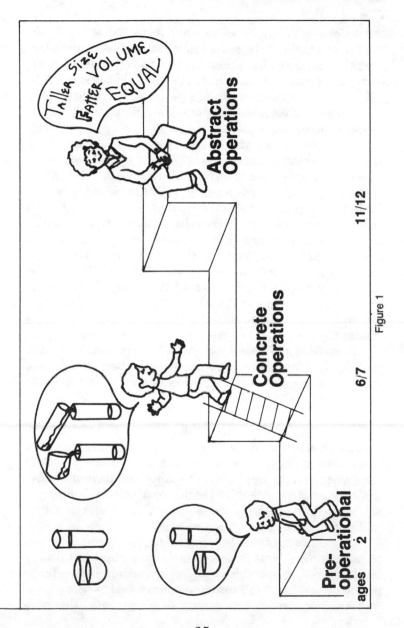

Figure 1

the water was the same height when it started he could pour it back and make it the same again, so it must be the same even though one looks higher. He begins to hold two aspects in mind; he can see that one glass is taller but also thinner. All these mental operations are performed on concrete objects only—the glasses and the water. Thus, we have the name "concrete operational" stage.

At about ages 11 and 12 the child enters the formal or abstract operational stage. This thinking continues to develop until about age 15. The child here can think about abstractions such as size, amount, tallness, shortness and so forth. He can perform mental operations on the abstractions and come to the conclusion that the water is the same. Thus, we call this the stage of formal operations. Thinking with abstractions enables the child to think beyond the present situation and form theories or generalizations about what happens when water is poured into differently shaped glasses, or about when any material changes its shape. This frees him from the *actual*; now all the *possible* is opened up to his thought.

In speaking of stages, we must be careful not to think that children jump from one to another on their birthdays or as a result of some clever teaching of ours. It is helpful to compare mental development with physical development. We often speak of "stages" of growth. We use terms such as toddlers, early childhood, middle childhood, and adolescence, but all of us can see that growth is continuous, and sometimes at the outer edges of our categories we are not sure what label to apply. For instance, we have difficulty drawing a hard and fast line which marks the beginning of adolescence. Sometimes we try to solve this problem by making a new category such as early adolescence.

Our concept of mental stages should resemble that of physical stages. This is particularly important at primary level where many children are in transition between the preoperational and the concrete operational stages.

Another caution concerning developmental theory is

that this does not mean we should turn our educational efforts toward moving children up the ladder of stages more rapidly. We need not bring glasses of water and pieces of clay into our classrooms and teach children how to perform in the Piaget experiments. This is what Piaget himself has to say about the question of acceleration.

> To be sure, all education in one way or another, is just such an acceleration, but it remains to be decided to what extent it is beneficial. It is not without significance that it takes man much longer to reach maturity than the other animals. Consequently, it is highly probable that there is an optimum rate of development, to exceed or fall behind which would be equally harmful. ("Forward" in *Learning and the Development of Cognition* by Barbel Inhelder et al. Cambridge: Harvard University Press, 1974, pp. 22-23.)

Rather than aiming to speed up development, a far more profitable route to take is to learn how best to teach at the different developmental levels. And that is what this book is largely about.

We will come back to some aspects of developmental theory and discuss them more fully. But first, let's take a look at two more theories that are having important influence on Christian education.

Behaviorist Theory

Behaviorism is almost synonymous with the name B. F. Skinner. In fact, we sometimes speak of Skinnerian psychology, or Skinnerism, but others through the years have also contributed to this theory.

Behaviorism does not view man as a biological organism, as developmental theory does, and it does not view him as a personality made in the image of God, as the Christian does. Behaviorists simply study behavior, and ignore what goes on in the "black box" of the mind. The hard-core behaviorists actually believe there is nothing in the black box that affects what comes out. There is no will, heart, personality, or spiritual self to initiate action. Only external factors count—stimuli, reward and punishment. These hard-core behaviorists are the people who believe we can eliminate crime by changing social conditions; criminal behavior is only the result of the environment.

For the behaviorist, a stimulus enters the black box and certain behavior results. Or a behavior that is rewarded will be "learned," by which is meant that it will be repeated, and a behavior that is not rewarded will be extinguished. Since science tries to deal with what is observable and measurable, behaviorists study the externals of responses and their contingencies. These are observable. Behaviorists count these, measure them, alter them, and develop systems to obtain predictable behaviors. We call this behavior modification.

Skinner has written, "The picture that emerges from a scientific analysis is not of a body with a person inside, but of a body which *is* a person in the sense that it displays a complex repertoire of behaviors . . . . Autonomous man is a device used to explain what we cannot explain in any other way. He has been constructed from our ignorance, and as our understanding increases, the very stuff of which he is composed vanishes." Continuing, Skinner describes an argument by Joseph Krutch in which "Hamlet articulates the traditional view of man by exclaiming, 'How like a god!' whereas Pavlov emphasized, 'How like a dog!'" Skinner comments, "But that was a step forward" (*Beyond Freedom and Dignity*, New York: Knopf, 1971, p. 201). Pavlov, of course, was the early behaviorist who "taught" dogs to salivate at the sound of a bell, by associating the bell with food for a time and later removing the food and using only the bell.

How does a behaviorist teach? First of all, he defines learning as being changed behavior. Usually he speaks of "modifying behavior." The dog "learned" when it salivated at the sound of the bell rather than at the sight or taste of food. This was a change, and thus a learning. So the behaviorist first identifies the behavior he wants changed. He specifies in exact terms whether he wants more or less of this behavior, how much more or less, and under what conditions. For instance, he will specify that the child will stay in his seat for a certain length of time or for a certain percentage of his school day. This becomes the behavioral objective. Then he manages the contingencies that follow the child's behavior. For this he uses punishment and reward. Reward may be smiles, praise, tokens to exchange for goodies or for free time, and so forth. Punishment is anything that reduces the behavior of getting out of the seat. By careful management of the contingencies, behavior is changed, and this is learning, by the behaviorist definition.

Some churches have adopted the token system. They give out tokens for good behavior on the bus or in class, and they operate a store where children can redeem their tokens. Teachers learn to reward behaviors they want with attention and praise and other means, and they learn to "punish" unwanted behavior by giving it no attention. Or if this is not possible, they scold or remove the child for a time from the group and so forth.

So teachers have adopted some practices of the behaviorists, but Christian teachers do not for a moment believe that this is all there is to learning. They cannot ignore the mind and heart of the child, and focus only on behaviors and changing them.

In view of the behaviorist origins of behavioral objectives, it is hard to understand why there is such a strong movement in Christian education today to use them. Some are insisting that every lesson ought to have a behavioral objective and that we ought to be able to measure what we have taught in terms of the changed behavior we accomplish. Perhaps some of this popularity stems from a misunderstanding of what it's all about. The technical idea of "behavioral objective" probably is translated in many teachers' minds to simply "behavior objective." In other words, they may be thinking of Christian behaviors they want their children to exhibit—kindness, obedience, accepting God's salvation, and so forth, and they overlook the whole system of reaching these objectives by managing the contingencies. Christians cannot ignore the black box of the mind. They cannot ignore heart. Christians believe that behavior comes out of the heart. It is the heart of the child that must be changed—not only the behavior.

Christians also believe that they should teach their children the Bible. Important knowledge is in the Bible for us. There God reveals what He is like. There He tells us how He made the world and mankind. He tells us of sin and salvation. He tells us of things to come. Some of these topics may seem to lend themselves to a behavioral objective—for instance, salvation. On a lesson about salvation an objective may be that the child will accept Christ as his Savior. At least this could be true on one lesson about salvation. After the child is saved, any further understanding about salvation would have to have another change of behavior as its objective. But even in this salvation example there are great differences between our Christian approach and the behaviorist approach. We believe salvation comes by a work of the Holy Spirit in the heart and we pray and teach toward this end. We do not concern ourselves with managing the contingencies of reward and punishment in order to bring about salvation.

If you meet a Christian educator who thinks he believes in behavioral objectives, try asking him this question: "What change of behavior do you expect from a lesson on creation?" His answer will probably be something like, "The child should worship the God who created all things." Next, you need to ask, "How do you observe and measure worship?" "Well, uh, the child will thank God for His great creation." Now, if you have only that little prayer sentence as your goal, that is easy to teach without bothering with the whole lesson on creation. Point that out to your behaviorist friend.

Of course, the behaviorist is in a trap here because his approach really should be to start from a behavior he wants changed. He should not be starting from Bible content—even so important a content as creation. If we were true behaviorists and started only from behavior we want to change, then planned contingencies for changing it, and measured the change, we would have an anemic Bible education, indeed.

But we are not true behaviorists. We know there are important revelations in God's Book that we need to teach. We know the child has a mind and heart for learning these, and he is not just a personless body. So, many of our attempts to incorporate something so foreign to our beliefs as behaviorism at best are ineffective and at worst are diluting and trivializing our teaching.

The best place for behavioral objectives is in skill areas and not in content areas. Finding Bible references and other Bible study skills and thinking skills, or beginning witnessing skills, lend themselves to behaviorally-stated objectives. Some of the tasks of Christian growth also can be stated as behavioral objectives. Knowledge goals put into behavioral form usually come out stating how the child will perform on a particular test. Deeper understandings, attitudes, and spiritual life goals can rarely be put into good form as behavioral objectives. Even when we do manage to get a well-stated behavioral objective, we do not use the rest of the behaviorist system—conditioning—to achieve the objective.

Those who are doing the best work along this line will be the first to tell you that they also aim for integrated thinking and understandings within the black box. They are using some of Skinner's ideas, but they are not Skinnerians in their view of man.

In summary, behaviorism is a scientific approach to the study of behavior, in which only exterior, observable factors are measured and studied. Any possible interior reasons for behavior are not considered. Some techniques and ideas developed from this theory can be used in Christian education in limited ways, but we cannot find in this theory an adequate psychological base for our educational program.

Needs Theory

Here is another theory that does not fully explain learning for us, but since it is so widely promoted in Christian education we will discuss it briefly here and try to understand what use we should make of it. By needs theory, we mean the idea proposed when it is said that every lesson should begin with a psychological need, or that no learning can take place without, in effect, being filtered through a need. All learning is seen as attempts to reduce needs. This theory is generally attributed to an early psychologist, Hull, and to Freud. But since it has not succeeded in predicting as a good theory should, it is not widely accepted today as The Way to learn.

Probably needs theory is best illustrated in the case of a troubled person who turns to the Bible to find some answer for his problem or some comfort to help in his distress. Youth leaders often take advantage of what they identify as common adolescent needs. For instance, they see loneliness as a common teenage problem, so they develop lessons or speeches around that topic. What happens in both these cases, is that the need serves as motivation for learning; it does not actually explain how learning takes place.

A primary teacher who believed in the needs theory said, "I find it's easy to teach to a child's needs. For instance I talk about being thirsty, and then I give the story of Ishmael in the desert." But a close look shows that this teacher is not actually meeting a child's need for water; she is, instead, catching his interest by using a common situation that all children can identify with.

A big problem in needs theory is identifying and agreeing on what every person's needs are. The most widely used list of needs is Abraham Maslow's, which in brief form looks like this.

1. Physiological needs (food, water, temperature regulation, etc.).
2. Safety needs (orderly, non-threatening environments).
3. Love and belonging needs (reciprocal relationships with others, membership in a group).
4. Self-esteem needs (recognition, achievement, self-worth).
5. Self-actualization needs (self-development and self-fulfillment).
6. Need to know and understand.

These needs are hierarchical, according to Maslow. That means that in general each higher order is built on what comes before. A child who has his physiological, safety, and love needs fairly well met will not have too much trouble building his self-esteem. But a child without the three lower needs met will have trouble with the fourth one. This feature of Maslow's theory is basic to understanding it. So the practice of adding "spiritual needs" to the top of Maslow's list makes no sense. It is incompatible with what Maslow is teaching us in his theory. It is not necessary to have the lower six needs fulfilled before a person begins trying to fulfill his spiritual need.

Maslow's theory is better called a theory of psychological development or of motivation. For a humanist, in which self-actualizing of the person is the sum total of learning and life, it can make a learning theory. But for a Christian it does not. Maslow was disenchanted with behaviorism with its dehumanizing influence. He repudiated orthodox science as The Path to knowledge. He saw man more wholistically. He saw him as dynamic, and not as simply responding to the environment. He studied humans, and not rats and pigeons as Skinner did. He studied healthy humans, and not abnormal ones as Freud did. In reading Maslow, one does feel much closer to a Christian view of man than in reading the behaviorists or the psychoanalysts, but his theory of psychological growth is not really a learning theory adequate for Christian education. Its best contribution is in the area of motivation. If you have a disruptive child, you may diagnose that he meets failure in his classwork but finds recognition from his peers by acting up. Your job then is to help him find recognition and achievement in his classwork. If you can manage this you will have motivated him to learn; his self-esteem needs will be met by his success in class.

But notice that the content of the child's learning in this case can be anything you want to teach him. You don't have to build your lessons around self-esteem in order to help this child. For all your children, you help meet the safety and love needs and other needs as well as you can, in numerous ways, such as in your relationships with them and in the way you structure the classroom environment. But you do not base your lesson content on these needs—except occasionally, as in the loneliness example given earlier. And you do not start each lesson by raising awareness of a psychological need you will meet as the lesson proceeds—only occasionally as you see fit.

A problem with the practice of using psychological needs as a basis for curriculum is that it assumes we have actually identified man's needs, and it ignores the possibility that God in His Word has given us what we need. Lessons and curriculum built around psychological needs would give us almost as anemic a Christian education as one built around behavioral objectives. Fortunately for Christian education, though this is much talked about, it is not often done. There are courses built around some of these ideas— such as "You Are Special" to try to meet the self-esteem need. But for the most part, teachers and curriculum planners believe first in teaching the Bible. Then those who think needs theory is The Path to learning try to cull from the Bible lesson some kind of need they can open the lesson with. Sometimes they are successful in finding an appropriate spiritual need which is pointed out in the Bible, rather than a psychological need, and the lesson works fine. But if you understand that this is not an essential part of the learning process you can free yourself to start off your lessons in a variety of ways.

Many people who talk about needs say they believe Maslow's list of psychological needs is the basis, or starting point, for learning. But if you press them for details and examples you find that they are not using Maslow's list at all. They use the word "needs" in a free way to refer to practically anything they think their students need to learn and any reason why they need to learn it. In this sense of the word we might say that all curriculum is based on need. But that is a theory of curriculum and not a theory of learning. It is not in any sense an explanation of how people learn.

In conclusion, Christian educators see these weaknesses in the needs theory of learning: 1) Lists of needs are psychological, and not spiritual, thus inadequate for Christian education, 2) the system is man-centered rather than God-centered, and 3) the theory fails to account for most learning.

Secular learning theories cannot give Christians The Formula for teaching. They do not allow place for our Biblical view of man with heart and soul and spirit. Even secular educators realize the shortcomings of these theories. Dr. Robert Coles writes, "I started out twenty years ago as a self-confident, smug theorist . . . . Today I am embarrassed. I am embarrassed by the preconceived notions I had . . . . I was assuming that the structure of the human mind had already been described, and my observations were just more grist for a mill already solidly in business" ("The Confessions of a Premier Child Specialist" in *Learning*, February 1979).

While we are not "solidly in business" in describing how children think and learn, we can gain many useful ideas from those who study the child mind. We turn now to some fascinating insights, first on concrete thinking, and next on poetic thinking. Neither of these traits are theories of learning as inclusive as, say, the developmental theory. They may be said to be related to developmental theory, and describe for us certain traits in the mental world of the primary child.

Concrete Thinking

What does it really mean to say that primary children think concretely? There is more to it than just that children might misunderstand the word heart, and think of the physical blood pump. Actually, this common example does not illustrate very well the concept of concreteness. This misunderstanding of heart happens occasionally in a child who has seen farm animals slaughtered or perhaps knows about the heart from a plastic model or some other source. But the large majority of children know heart from valentines or songs long before they meet the physical organ. So teaching children who think concretely is not accomplished simply by avoiding the word heart and other similar words.

Looking at some of the children's own remarks will help to make clear what their concrete thinking is like, so we present here several interviews with primary children. In the first two, the interviewer is trying to get at the children's concept of "family." Children's thinking is not always apparent in the first answers they give us, as you will notice in these two interviews. Both Jenny and Shelley give practically the same answer when the question is first posed, but as the interviewer probes further you begin to see an enormous difference. Jenny sees family quite concretely; it is the people who live together in one house. Shelley's idea of family transcends the group housed together physically in one place; she struggles also with the relationships of marriage and birth.

Interview with Jenny, age 6:4.

I: Do you know the word family? What does family mean?

J: A whole bunch of people.

I: Do you have a family?

J: Mm-hmm.

I: Who are the people in your family?

J: Mother and father.

I: And anybody else?

J: Two brothers.

I: And anybody else?

J: Me.

I: Does your daddy have a family?

J: Yes, grandma and grandpa.

I: Do you know if he has any sisters?

J: He does.

I: Do you know how many there are?

J: Six.

I: Do you know how many brothers he has?

J: No. Probably just one.

I: Well, all those people in your daddy's family—are they in your family?

J: (Shakes head No.)

I: Why not?

J: Because . . .

I: Because. Any other reasons?

J: Because they don't live with us.

I: Oh. Would they be part of your family if they came and lived with you?

J: (Nods Yes.)

Interview with Shelley, age 7:6.

I: What does the word family mean?

S: Means a whole bunch of people that live together in a house.

I: Do you have a family?

S: Mm-hmm.

I: Can you tell me about your family? Who are the people in your family?

S: My mommy is in my family and she cooks the supper. And my daddy gets money from work. And then me and Karen—my sister Karen—play games and Monopoly and stuff, and Michael likes to get in there and bother us. And Bonnie always takes the stuff that we're playing with and scatters them all over the place.

I: Does your daddy have a family?

S: Mm-hmm.

I: Who is your daddy's mother?

S: Grandmother.

I: Now, is your daddy's family part of your family?

S: Mm-hmm.

I: Why is that?

S: Because my daddy got married to my mommy, and my mommy had us and then our daddy would be part of, part of the family. Well, we'd be part of his family because we're in his family.

I: Are you part of your mother's family?

S: Uh-huh.

I: Why is that?

S: Because my mother was married to my father and then we are in my mother's family.

I: Is that why you're in your mother's family? Because your mother married your father?

S: No.

I: Is there more reason? Another reason?

S: I don't know very much about families because we don't learn that in school. But I know lots about frogs.

Jenny shows what most of your younger primary children are like. Shelley is rather advanced for her age, and her view shows the level some of your older primary children may reach.

Here are the same two girls again, being interviewed concerning their idea of "promise." They have just heard the story of Linda, adapted from the filmstrip "You Promised" by Guidance Associates. Linda's friend's kitten is up a tree and can't get down. Linda, being the best climber in the neighborhood, is the only one who can save the kitten. But she has promised her father she will not climb trees. The interviews have been shortened some from the original tapes, but the questions and answers which do appear are complete; no words are changed.

Interview with Jenny.

I: What do you think Linda should do?

J: Go up and get that cat and take it to her friend's house.

I: Why should she do that?

J: Because he might—she might be lost.

I: The kitten might be lost, you mean?

J: Yeah.

I: Well, what about the promise she made to her daddy about not climbing trees?

J: If she'd ask someone else she can.

I: Well, what's going to happen when her daddy finds out?

J: She'll get a spanking.

I: And so you think she should climb up and get the kitten?

J: (Shakes head No.)

I: You think she shouldn't get the kitten? Why shouldn't she?

J: Because her dad said not to.

I: Well, what will happen to the kitten if she doesn't climb up?

J: The cat will never find its way down.

I: That would be kind of sad. Do you think Linda should just leave the kitty up there?

J: (Nods head Yes.)

I: You think it is more important for Linda to keep her promise to her daddy?

J: Uh-huh.

I: And it's not more important to save the kitty?

J: No.

I: Why?

J: Because her dad said not to climb up on the tree.

Interview with Shelley.

I: What should Linda do?

(Shelley suggests getting her daddy, mother, fire-
men and others, but the interviewer says this is
impossible.)

I: What if she just couldn't get help any way?

S: She would climb the tree and then when her father
got home she should tell him that she had to get the kitty
down.

I: And then what? What should the father do then?

S: Spank her . . . the father should tell her that it was
good that she saved the kitty but she wasn't supposed to do
that.

I: So you think the father would have just kind of
talked to her like that and . . .

S: So he would be really mad and have a frown on his
face.

I: Do you think he would punish her? Do you think he
should punish her?

S: Well, if she was saving an animal's life I don't think
he should punish her because God made the animals and
God wants the animals to be alive that He makes.

I: And how do you think the father would feel about
Linda breaking a promise?

S: Well . . . he would sort of feel a little bit on the not
quite sure side.

I: Not quite sure about what?

S: He's not sure that she should have done that.

I: Oh.

S: But he still was sort of proud of her for getting the
kitty out of the tree.

I: Oh. Okay, do you think it's ever all right then to
break a promise?

S: Well, if you're saving somebody's life or an animal's

life it would be okay. But if you weren't, if you were just doing it for fun it wouldn't be okay.

In these interviews you notice that Jenny did a 180 degree turn. She wanted Linda to save the kitten as much as Shelley did, and that was the aspect that she "centered" on at the first. But when she was reminded of the promise, she centered on it and her answer changed. She had no way in her thinking yet to weigh one value against another—to operate on two elements and come to a conclusion or decision about them. You might say that for Jenny a promise is a promise is a promise and nothing more can be said. Jenny appears to be at the preoperational level.

Shelley is at the concrete operational level. She could weigh the value of a kitten's life against a broken promise and make her decision. This is a mental operation on two concrete elements. (Promise in a generalized sense could be an abstraction, but in the context of this story it is concrete; Shelley is thinking about this particular promise.) Once the decision was made, the broken promise loomed up rather concretely and she felt that naturally it deserved a spanking. But then she seemed to realize that the father would understand—he would not think so concretely—and she decided he would merely frown and not spank.

Shelley's comment about God creating the kitten shows a remarkably high level of insight for a primary child. This is an example of basing action upon a principle, and many adults do not do that. Many people go through life in what can be called a "law stage." They do right because it is the law or rule. But Shelley in this instance would do what she thinks is right because she believes in a high principle.

Dilemmas, such as the Linda story, where there is a difficult choice and something seems "wrong" either way, are sometimes used in teaching and research in moral development. But for Christians there is a flaw in this technique, since the children are allowed no third option. They can't say, for instance, that Linda should pray and ask God for help; He would show her some way so she would not have to break her promise. The interviews are given here simply as examples of concrete thinking.

Poetic Thinking

> Wynken, Blynken, and Nod one night
>   Sailed off in a wooden shoe—
> Sailed on a river of crystal light,
>   Into a sea of dew.

Eugene Field made the words float around your ears; they sail and rock on the waves, just like the boat. He doesn't say to you, "Now I'm going to make some words that will rock you off to sleep." He says instead, "The old moon laughed and sang a song, As they rocked in the wooden shoe, And the wind that sped them all night long Ruffled the waves of dew." The similarity, or the analogy, of his words with a wave-tossed boat is there for all to enjoy, but only a few people analyze this as one of the reasons why the words are so powerful. Field himself tells us some other analogies: "The little stars are the herring fish That lived in that beautiful sea" and "Wynken and Blynken are two little eyes, And Nod is a little head, And the wooden shoe that sailed the skies Is a wee one's trundle-bed."

Analogy is at the heart of poetic thinking, and at the heart of creativity. Field's creative genius here was to develop the image of the wooden-shoe boat sailing the night skies and to use it as a picture of the child going off to sleep.

Now let's look at a portion of "The Hound of Heaven" by Francis Thompson. Thompson does not explain for us his analogies, as Field did, but when we see his use of the word "pulled," along with a derivation of "pillar," we can't help but see a Samson-like tragedy in these lines.

> In the rash lustihead of my young powers,
>   I shook the pillaring hours

> And pulled my life upon me; grimed with smears,
> I stand amid the dust o' the mounded years—
> My mangled youth lies dead beneath the heap.

You may want to read this a couple more times to see things you missed the first time. The image here—the analogy—has a power that is lost when we try to translate it into the bare bones of prosaic meaning. We could say it means, "My life was wasted," but much meaning as well as power is lost in this translation.

A psychologist early in the century said that children think like poets. By this he meant that their minds leap directly across analogies without stopping to analyze them. In our day, Piaget has used the word "transductive" to describe this same phenomenon in children of the preoperational stage.

This is not to say that children have a genius for being poets that we adults have lost. It is simply to say that they can derive meaning without having to go through our adult logical processes. In the story of the lost sheep, if it is told from the point of view of the sheep, children can identify with the sheep, and the meaning of "lostness" and of being found comes through even if they do not make the analogy of "sheep equals me." If the story is told from the point of view of the shepherd (as Jesus tells it) the meaning of love and seeking come through even if children do not dissect the analogy of "shepherd equals Jesus." For a long time children think Jesus *is* the shepherd, rather than thinking that Jesus loves as a shepherd loves.

This direct, unanalyzed thinking of the early years is probably the source—at least one source—of the power of early learning. Such images ingested at an early age, with all the accompanying emotional meaning, are practically impossible to erase at later ages. If someone comes along later with adult logic and says, "God doesn't have time to worry about little individuals like us," he is not likely to influence one who learned his Bible stories early in life.

In the story of the potter and the pot, few primary children will be able to analyze and say the potter stands for God, and the pot stands for the nation (or me). But there is much meaning in the story for these children anyway. The potter is working and working on a pot. He wants to make it beautiful, but he finds a flaw; the pot is cracked. So he smashes it and starts all over again and at last his pot is finished—flawless and beautiful. The power of the potter over his own clay is evident. Of course he can smash it if he wants to. His concern that the pot be perfect, and his ability to make it so, also come through to children as meanings. The view of the clay can also be seen. "Ouch, it hurts to smash me up." But the happy ending is that it comes out looking more beautiful than ever, and now it can be used.

Developmental theory shows us that logical reasoning arrives usually after the primary years. So some people are saying we should delay much of our Bible teaching until the age when children can "understand" it. But much understanding is not coldly logical. Much of it is concrete, poetic, intuitive. Here lies the power of the young child's mind. The primary child needs Bible stories before he loses this power.

READING CHECK

1. Developmental theory describes for us **how** children think rather than **what** they think.   T   F

2. We now know that we should wait until children outgrow the preoperational stage before teaching them Bible stories.   T   F

3. Behaviorist theory describes for us **what** children think rather than **how** they think.   T   F

4. Behaviorists view man as an organism that responds to and is manipulated by environment.   T   F

5. Behavioral objectives are an outgrowth of behaviorist theory.   T   F

6. Every good lesson plan must have a behavioral objective.   T   F

7. Every good lesson plan must start with a need.   T   F

8. We can reach children better if we view their concrete thinking as a powerful attribute and not as a deficiency.   T   F

9. With primary children we should avoid Bible stories based on analogy.   T   F

10. Concrete teaching means you must have objects or visuals for primaries to manipulate.   T   F

Answers: 1—T, 2—F, 3—F (It describes neither of these), 4—T, 5—T, 6—F, 7—F, 8—T, 9—F, 10—F (This is more necessary at preoperational level than at the concrete operational level.)

3 Bible Learning

- *The Expurgated Bible*
- *Doctrine*
- *Reading the Bible*

The Expurgated Bible

Many of us now living have seen stories change in our own lifetime. The wolf does not eat Grandmother anymore so that the woodsman has to cut the beast open and free the dear old woman. Instead, the wolf merely runs off to the woods and is never seen again. Would that evil could be disposed of so easily. Rhymes, too, have been reformed. In "Ding Dong Bell" there is no naughty boy who puts a cat down a well, and even the cat unnaturally eats no mice. The Millenium must be here.

> Ding Dong bell, Pussy's at the well.
> Who took her there? Little Johnny Hare.
> Who'll bring her in? Little Tommy Thin.
> What a jolly boy was that to get some milk for pussycat,
> Who ne'er did any harm, but played with the mice in his father's barn.

We seem to believe that childhood is all innocence and sweetness and light—or should be. We have made childhood a time to learn that God is good and loving and kind. There's time enough later—we think—to learn about evil and God's judgment. We teach that God made the world good; little children in flower-strewn fields chasing butterflies is too often our picture of the world. We fail to add with sufficient emphasis that sin has brought a curse on the world, and cats do eat mice, and men are killed. Death, judgment, evil—these realities we attempt to save for a later time.

We may have thought in earlier days that we were being "psychologically sound" in sparing our children a view of the evils of life and giving them only sweetness. But recently too many psychiatrists and psychologists have been saying otherwise, so that we no longer can use that reason. Giants and monsters and other frightening things have been in the world's literature for as long as we know. And now our scholars of the mind are showing us how the old tales help children face and conquer the giants within them. The whole world loves the story of David and Goliath. Wouldn't everyone like to conquer his troubles as bravely as David did? It is only a Sunday school teacher who can raise the question, "Should we teach children to kill?"

This kind of Bible teacher can get by the story of Noah and the flood by making it a charming story of a quaint old boat, a menagerie of animals, and a beautiful rainbow; the millions of dying people are passed over. But God's judgment in some stories is not so easily passed over. Korah, Nadab and Abihu, Ananias and Sapphira—these stories, such a teacher has to omit. She does not want to teach that God is like that.

But God *is* like that. Better to learn it from the old Bible stories than to learn it on Judgment Day. This is not to argue for frightening children in our Sunday school classes. No, we need to handle such stories carefully. The child can feel safety in knowing that the teacher is in control in class and God is in control in the world. God gets rid of evil in these stories; He wants only good. How comforting to be on God's side.

A psychiatric view is that many children invent their own horrors of the mind—their bogy men and murderers and mutilators. They do this whether they have heard frightening stories or not. If no adult will admit to this, the child is left to face his fears (his sin?) alone. But stories help to bring these fears out of the mind and into the open.

Bible stories help children sort out the realities of life. There is both good and evil. God is the Author of good. He is more powerful than anything, and He will win in the end. This world view helps a child much more than a view which seems to deny until he is ten years old or so that evil exists.

The Bible stories make abstractions concrete. There is sharp contrast and visible difference between good and evil—between those who obey God and those who do not; some people are saved in the ark and some are drowned in the flood. In Moses' day the children must have seen much of the slaughtering of animals; sacrifice for sins was vivid and concrete to them. When the earth opened to swallow Korah and his followers, God did not say, "Take all the children away first; I don't want them to see this." When Achan was stoned to death the children may not have been there because it was a military situation, but the mound remained as a "memorial" for a long time after, and many children must have seen that and asked about it.

Some may say, "But that was Old Testament; it is different now." What is different? God is never-changing. Even the Old Testament says, "He has not dealt with us after our sins; nor rewarded us according to our iniquities" (Psalm 103:10), so we see God's mercy in Old Testament times. And even the New Testament has the Ananias and Sapphira story so we see God bringing sudden judgment in New Testament times. We can say we are under grace and not under law, but God's holiness and His hatred of sin are the same. Jesus took the penalty of our sin upon Him, and the Bible stories of God's judgment on sin help us appreciate more fully what the Lord did for us in His death on the cross.

God is the same, so what is different? Children? Are our children different than Moses' and Joshua's children? No, they still have the same need to know God. They still are born with Adam's sin in their natures.

What is different, perhaps, is our culture and our view of children. Many cultures of the world do not segregate children so much and insulate them from the adult world. But in our society we do. And we have listened to psychologists with a Rousseau-like, romantic view of the child as a flower which can only grow good unless we tell it about evil. Our view of the flowers is fading, though, and our children are seeing much evil and violence on TV and elsewhere. And it may be partly in reaction to this that Sunday school teachers object to "violence" in Bible stories.

But we need to see the essential difference between TV violence and that found in some Bible stories. Bible stories are always full of meaning. Death, for instance, comes at the end of a long, faithful life, and it is a beautiful occasion of finishing a well-lived life and moving on to something better; or else it is a judgment for sin. Wars, murders, calamities and other violence are seen from God's view. Children learn truth from the Bible stories. Truth may not always be pleasant and sweet, but it is always good.

TV violence, on the other hand, is shown for the "entertainment" value of the violent acts themselves. The aim often is to elicit the tense, horror-stricken grip that keeps people glued to the set to see what will happen next. There is usually no moral value at all. It is difficult for children even to know who are the good guys or the bad guys, since several killings may take place before it is established who the bad guys are.

The Bible stories do not dwell on a violent act itself, but on purposes and eternal truths. There is moral value in these stories, and spiritual learning. They are rich in meaning. None of this can be said of most TV stories. Bible stories and even fairy tales read or told to children have still other differences from stories viewed on TV. They are heard in the safe presence of a trusted adult. The adult can temper the story if a child is too affected by it. He stops after a story or two and does not go endlessly on as TV does. The child makes his own images of a story he is hearing, and since he makes them they are images he can cope with. But with TV he has images thrust upon him which he often is not able to cope with adequately.

So considering all these differences, violence itself is not an important reason for omitting certain stories from the primary child's Bible. But there are some other reasons why you may want to skip a story. One reason might be that the story illustrates truths too difficult for primaries to understand or truths you consider not appropriate or useful for primary age children.

And some stories have content which is inappropriate or not understandable to primaries. Stories of sex sins will often fall into this category. Even though our society teaches sex earlier and earlier, this is not always as successful as we hope, and not as needed as we think. There is the first grader who came home from school and asked, "Mom, where did I come from?" Mom had prepared for this moment, and she gave a long explanation, after which her son said, "That's funny. Billy came from New York." Many children, as this one, do not need or want sex information as early as they get it. And in our Bible teaching we leave much of this out not only because we feel it imprudent, but also because young children do not understand it.

In summary, we choose some stories and pass over others when planning for primary children. But we need to be careful not to omit too much, or to omit stories for the wrong reasons. If we do, we are in danger of giving children a lopsided view of God and of other important learnings.

Doctrine

Primary children can learn a great deal about the major doctrines of the Bible if these teachings are given to them in appropriate concrete form. There really is almost no important Bible topic that primary children cannot learn at their level of understanding. And they should learn them during these years. A good grounding at the concrete level is essential for later understanding at an abstract level.

There is no merit in waiting until children are more fully developed intellectually before teaching them basic Bible doctrines. As children learn at one level they develop intellectually, then they are able to learn at a higher level, and so forth. This "spiraling" learning should continue all through the growing years if we want our children to grasp the Bible in any cohesive way.

Following, are some important doctrinal topics, that children can be learning during primary years.

God. Children think of God as a person who can do anything. God made everything, God hears our prayers, God watches over us, and so forth. They think God's home is in Heaven, but they do not have much problem believing that God can live in us, too. The best way to be concrete in teaching about God, is to use Bible stories which show something God does. The ladder of abstraction below will illustrate this.

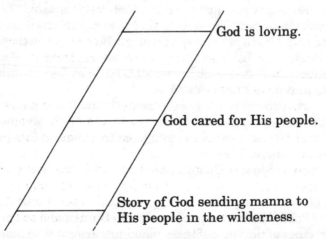

God is loving.

God cared for His people.

Story of God sending manna to His people in the wilderness.

The story of manna is one specific incident in which God showed His love. A specific incident is concrete. If we say, "God cared for His people in the wilderness," we have included many other actions of God along with the manna one, and have abstracted only the common element, caring. Notice, we do not have all the concrete items enumerated here. For us as adults and Bible teachers much of this concrete knowledge is stored away in our memories and our understanding. We also know from other contexts the kinds of things that can be included under the abstraction "care." Such background is what helps us know the meaning of the statement on Step 2 of the ladder. Children have less background for this, and thus a lesser understanding of the statement.

On the third step we generalize from still a wider range of God's actions—those in which He guides, teaches, forgives, and others, as well as those in which He cared in a physical way. We also have included a wider range of peoples and places. But we have abstracted from the "caring" idea only an attribute of God which we feel helps account for His caring. We have omitted God's actions and His relationships with the people.

Each step up the ladder includes everything below, and much more. But each step up the ladder abstracts a smaller and smaller portion of any one original concrete happening. With primaries we stay as close to the bottom of the ladder as possible. It takes numerous concrete learnings to build up the meanings of abstractions.

This does not mean we avoid the word *love* because it is an abstraction, but it means we should tie it to concrete incidents. God loved these people, at this time, in this place, in this way.

So in teaching about God we will use many Bible stories. Children can learn that God spoke commandments to Moses, He made an earthquake swallow rebellious Korah and his followers, He gave visions to Daniel, and so on. But all these concrete incidents should not be in a haphazard mixture; children will not be able to organize meaning by themselves. It is up to curriculum planners to do the organizing. Adults who know the important Bible doctrines of God need to guide the children in this learning and help them see what God is like, as they meet Him over and over in the stories.

Jesus. Stories about what Jesus did and what Jesus said will teach in a concrete way that Jesus is kind, loving, powerful, and any other attributes you wish to teach. The ladder again shows how this works.

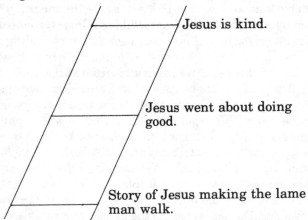

Jesus is kind.

Jesus went about doing good.

Story of Jesus making the lame man walk.

Step 1 is a concrete, specific happening. Step 2 abstracts from this incident only the idea of doing good. The lameness, the walking, and the man himself are omitted. Step 3 omits the actions of Jesus and abstracts only an attribute which was shown in those actions.

Both this ladder and the previous one show why children have difficulty thinking in terms of attributes. Much research on how children think of God has also shown this. Children can more easily answer the question "What did Jesus (or God) do?" than the question "What is Jesus (or God) like?" We should teach in verbs instead of adjectives.

We can also try nouns. They are more difficult than verbs, but easier than adjectives. Especially in teaching about Jesus, we seem to need nouns. We want to teach that Jesus is the Son of God or that He is our Savior. At first children use these terms simply as names for Jesus, and we have to add meaning piece by piece in concrete ways.

Primary children can learn that Jesus created every-thing, He lived in Heaven with God, He came to earth as a baby, He never sinned but He died for our sins, He came to life again and went back to live in Heaven, He is getting a place ready for us, He will come again someday and rule over all the world. These are all verbs. They are things Jesus did or will do.

During the primary years, children should learn a great deal about Jesus.

The Holy Spirit. We have fewer stories about the Holy Spirit, but we should use them and teach of the Holy Spirit in the same concrete manner. The major story, of course, is Pentecost when the Holy Spirit came and tongues of fire alighted on each person present. The Holy Spirit alighted as a dove on Jesus at His baptism. It seems as though we all need some concrete teaching of the Holy Spirit, and God has given it to us in these forms. We can pass these stories on to the children even if we don't know exactly what to make of the fire and the dove.

We should also use stories of people and what they did after the Holy Spirit came upon them or dwelt in them. Gideon, Peter, and John are some examples.

Sin and Salvation. Children all know sin from their own experiences, but they may not know what to call it. Children know inside themselves when they are being naughty, disobedient, rebellious. We need to help them attach the word *sin* to acts that are sinful. When the Israelites made a golden calf and bowed down to it, that was sin. When Ananias told a lie, that was sin. Stories of modern day children, as well as Bible stories, can also help us teach about sin, confessing it, and asking for forgiveness.

Many children can be saved at primary ages. In fact, these years may be the best time for well-taught children to come to Christ. The older idea that junior years are the best for this, was likely a self-fulfilling prophecy. That is, since we were accustomed to thinking of this period as the time to be saved, we geared our teaching to this and it did in fact come true. But with proper teaching, these statistics can be reversed. One teacher of second grade saw eleven of her twelve pupils come to Christ. A pastor said, "It used to be my junior children who were saved, but now hardly a Sunday goes by without one or more of my primaries tugging at my coat and telling me they were saved in Sunday school class." These results came from teaching salvation in primary classes, and from teaching it on the children's concrete level.

To be concrete in teaching about salvation, the best way is to use Bible stories. Adam and Eve sinned and God had to kill an animal to provide covering for them; sinners need a covering. God accepted Abel's lamb (and not Cain's offering) because blood sacrifice is necessary for sinners. Abraham was about to offer Isaac to God but God provided a ram to die in his place. Jesus died on the cross in our place. These and other such Bible stories provide vivid, clear, concrete teaching. They "show" instead of "tell" about God's way of salvation. (For an example of a primary course that uses this plan, see *God Gives Me Salvation*, Accent-B/P Publications.)

When children know they are sinners and when they know God's way of salvation, they can be saved. There is "human meaning" in the need to be saved from sin. This does not require understanding a chain of formal logic: Adam sinned, *therefore* all are sinners, *therefore* I am a sinner. Children simply come to know within themselves that they are sinners; this is the human condition. Neither does it require formal logic to understand the way of salvation: sin deserves death, and I am a sinner, therefore I deserve death, and so forth, down to receiving God's gift of salvation. Formal logic is a way we think sometimes when we are older. But children can know these things directly, from the stories which show them so concretely.

Concerning the procedures to use in handling individual decisions, teachers have been successful with a variety of approaches. Most, perhaps, try to leave the initiative up to the child, encouraging them to come to the teacher or to someone else when they want to be saved. This way they feel they can be more sure the children's decisions are genuine.

Sometimes teachers show a whole class how to come to the Lord, asking forgiveness, receiving Jesus, thanking Him for the gift of salvation. The teacher actually leads in prayer a phrase at a time, and suggests that those who want to can pray the same thing after her, either silently or aloud.

The group procedure is really not any more likely than the individual one to give children a false assurance of salvation. Both procedures could lead to such false assurance, but neither one needs to. It is all in the way you handle it. Before group prayer, you should introduce it as an opportunity to be saved or as a teaching on how to be saved, not as The Thing itself. In other words, you will not say, "How many want to be saved? Okay, I see your hands. Now, bow your heads and say these words after me." And you will not say after the prayer that now the children are saved, Jesus is living in their hearts, and so forth.

Instead, you will make every effort to teach that this is something between God and each individual. When your class is talking about salvation, when they perhaps have just had a story about the jailor being saved, or another salvation lesson, the conversation can lead naturally to the question of how we go about it when we want to be saved. Then you can tell the children that we talk to God about it, and you will show them how. "If you want to be saved right now you can talk to God yourself while I help you." After the prayer you can discuss how God knows and each child knows whether he really is saved. Just saying the words didn't do it but the children must really mean what they pray. Explain that if they weren't saved just now they can be anytime they want; they can talk to God anytime, anywhere, and be saved.

This last, is one value of group prayer. It helps teach the children how to talk to God about salvation. If this is always handled in individual conferences with the teacher, it can become a little like secret initiation rites into the "club." A good many children, of course, do receive Christ as they talk and pray with their teachers in private conferences. But children should know that this is not the only way.

Whether you are talking with individuals or with groups it is always wise to avoid telling a child outright that now he is saved. In some cases he may not be. The child should be the one who begins to tell it. Primaries can learn from Romans 10:9 and 10 that this is what they should do.

Some teachers reading this book who are inexperienced in all this may be hoping for an actual sample prayer to use. There sometimes is controversy over what are the "right" words to use. Some would insist that you cannot just receive God's free gift of salvation in a prayer time, but you first have to ask forgiveness for your sins. And you can't just say you're *sorry* for your sins because that meaning is not quite right; the really Biblical thing is to *repent*. Most of this hair-splitting is inappropriate at primary level because these children don't attach our adult meanings to words anyway. When the Holy Spirit is dealing with a child He works through the heart, and our words are not that critical. So your prayer can be in words you feel your children understand. It can include 1) asking forgiveness, 2) receiving Christ, and 3) thanking God for salvation. Sometimes it is a good plan to have conversation about each part of the prayer just before praying it.

A salvation prayer which follows a Bible story can take on the wording of the particular story. For instance, after the story of the Philippian jailor the children can tell God that they believe on the Lord Jesus Christ and can thank Him that Jesus died for them. After the story of Adam and Eve's sin they can tell God that they are sinners too and can thank the Lord for dying to be their covering for sin.

Your patient, thorough teaching will help the children become more and more familiar with the terms salvation, confess, repent, forgive, eternal life, sinner, believe, sacrifice, shed blood, and others that we use in talking about this topic. The best way to learn these is in context—in stories and in life. Children need to meet these words many times in many places. They need to hear them, read them, talk about them, think about them, pray them. Children do not learn words upon one meeting. Primary years are ideal for learning about all of these.

Heaven, Hell and Death. Children's understanding of death has been studied by psychologists, and the general finding is that by age 6 children have a pretty good understanding of it—not yet a full understanding in all respects, but good enough that we need not avoid the topic. (The development of this concept is described in more detail in the kindergarten book of this series.)

Children's writers have found the topic of death again after a silence of some decades, so there are a number of books out now purporting to help children cope with death. Secular attempts at this are pathetic when viewed by a Christian. Billy searches for meaning when his beloved dog dies. One "meaning" that is supposed to comfort him is that the dog goes into the ground and helps other things to grow. In other words he becomes fertilizer. Sammy's little sister won't feel anything when she is put into the ground; that is just her body. The part of her that dreams goes "somewhere else." A moth flies out the window of his sister's room and he imagines her spirit flying out. Often in these stories, someone's spirit living on simply means that that person has influenced those still living; his "spirit" lives on in them. The stories sometimes have a poetic beauty that masks their emptiness.

How rich a teaching we can give our children in comparison to the non-Christian! Death for the Christian is moving from this life to the eternal life with God where there is no more death. We think it's sad when someone dies, but God and the angels are happy to welcome the new one home. We think it's especially sad when someone dies young, and we don't know why it happens, but God knows. He always has a good reason. We can think of the loved one as happy with the Lord in Heaven—not as "somewhere else," or as living on in us, or as fertilizer. We can expect to see the loved one someday when we ourselves die and go to Heaven.

Death, for Christians, is not the worst thing that can happen, as it so often is for others. It is worse to be unfaithful to God, to take the wrong side. Right and truth have more value than life. Stephen died because he followed the Lord, and many Christians today are just as heroic.

Of course death does not always mean going to Heaven. Those who do not belong to God, go to Hell and everlasting punishment. Children should know this, too. They need to grow up with this as part of the fabric of their thinking. It should be right there, along with Heaven and God and everlasting life. It is important that children not get a lopsided view of such basic Christian teachings. If they are given the complete story in the beginning, they will grow into fuller understanding as their minds grow, and they will not have to relearn or unlearn later in life.

The Bible. Sometimes a teacher holds up a Bible and says, "This is the Word of God." We talk about God's Book, God's Word, or God's words. The names we use help to teach that the Bible is a special book, different from ordinary books. But we can go much further than this. As with other Bible doctrines, we can use stories in the Bible itself to help develop meaning behind the term "God's Word." We can make the teachings concrete by showing some of the ways God gave His words to us in the Bible.

On the mountain, God wrote the ten commandments with His own finger, and He told Moses other things to write down also. God touched Jeremiah's mouth and gave him words which his scribe wrote down. God gave visions to Daniel, and Daniel wrote them for us to read. Luke wrote stories about Jesus and the apostles—stories of things which really happened.

With these and other such concrete examples of how our Bible came to be, the children will gradually build up meaning for the term "God's Word." We may think of God's Word abstractly, as God's communication to mankind. But the children need to build up to this understanding incident by concrete incident. The primary years are the proper time for this careful, systematic building of meanings.

Other Doctrines. All other doctrines should be approached in the same concrete manner suggested for those doctrines already discussed. Children can easily learn of angels by what they do in the Bible stories. They also can learn of Satan and his demons. In our day it is especially important that children learn of these evil beings from godly teachers who will present them in proper perspective. If they don't, many are likely to learn of them from other children with unhealthy curiosity in the spirit world, who dabble with ouija boards and other dangerous practices.

Doctrines of future things are also easy to teach primary children. Simply use the Bible stories of what is going to happen. In this area there is much more detail than most children are interested in or could possibly absorb. But the great themes of Jesus' return, of His righteous reign on earth, of Satan's ultimate destruction, and of eternity with the Lord, should become part of the fabric of every child's thinking.

This rounds out his cosmic view. He then knows the beginning of things and the ending of things. He has a framework for history and it will shape all his learning that follows.

Doctrines of the church, which may seem simple since the church is so close to us, actually are some of the most difficult to teach at primary age. The main reason for this is the lack of Bible stories which make the teaching concrete. Most Bible teaching on the church is found in New Testament letters, and contains abstract concepts such as grafting the church in the place of Israel, and the church as the body of Christ. There are only a few stories to use. One notable one is the church at Jerusalem sending out missionaries and hearing the report when they came back. This shows the church as a missionary agency. Other stories can show the birth of the church and planting of local churches. A primary child's teaching on church will come partly from what he learns of his own church.

Reading the Bible

Alone in a storefront building the inner city Sunday school worker was straightening things up. In walked a child from the street.

"Hello," she said. "I'm Mrs. Hawkins. Who are you?"

"Tony."

A few more pleasantries were exchanged. Mrs Hawkins continued her work, and Tony took a Bible from the shelf and sat by a table to read it.

Mrs. Hawkins watched out of the corner of her eye. "He's such a little tyke," she thought. "Can't be more than second grade." She waited a bit, then decided to ask, "Can you read that?"

"Sure."

"How about reading some for me?" She left her work and sat down beside him.

He read a bit, not stumbling at all at the *thees* and *thous* or *believeths* of the King James Version, and even managing the word *resurrection*.

"What grade are you in?"

"Third." That meant he would be starting third grade in a couple of weeks.

"Where did you learn to read the Bible like that?"

"Mrs. Moreno taught me."

Mrs. Moreno was a former worker at the Sunday school. She evidently had not wasted her energy lamenting, "Why don't they teach 'em to read these days?"

This familiar lament is not unique to Sunday school teachers, but high school teachers want to know why they don't teach 'em better in elementary school. Elementary teachers want to know why they don't teach 'em better in preschool. And preschool teachers have only the parents to pass the blame to.

In Bible teaching it is a mistake to wait until the public schools have prepared children to read the Bible. Many sixth graders without Bible background (King James) have no idea what *thou* means. Even when the word is seen in context in a sentence some will not hazard a guess about its meaning. And if you wait for the schools to teach *propitiation* you would wait forever.

Bible teachers must incorporate some reading instruction along with other teaching. This is true at all levels (even many adults do not know whether to say HAbakkuk or HaBAKkuk), but at primary level it is more important than ever.

There is nothing at all mysterious about teaching reading. Teachers read every day of their lives. They know this skill better than many skills they use and teach. Yet when faced with the prospect of teaching it many are fearful.

When you learned to drive a car someone showed you certain moves to make. You may or may not have understood what happened to the inner workings of the car when you turned the steering wheel. You may or may not have understood anything about gears beyond the lever or the buttons that you pushed. As the years passed and you had various mechanical problems with your cars you learned more. There was nothing systematic about it; you just learned as the occasion arose.

Reading can be that way. You can teach a word whole: "This word is *God*." Or you can at times point out one detail of it: "The word that starts with *M* is *Moses*." Children build up their reading skills bit by little bit, so you are teaching reading any time you add a bit to their learning.

Reading has become an emotional topic in our day and phonics has been fought over until some people believe the child is not actually reading until he can sound out every letter. Some even go so far as to believe the child will not understand the word unless he has sounded it out. In the auto illustration, you may not fully understand your car's workings, but you use what you do know in your driving and care for the car and diagnosing of its symptoms. Likewise, children, when they do not fully understand the phonics system, can use what they do know.

Growing in reading ability is exciting for most primary children. We should capitalize on this high interest and make good use of it in Bible teaching. Sunday schools which do this well throughout the primary years will have children who can study from their own Bibles much earlier. And they are not so likely to have junior teachers who say, "Why don't they teach 'em in primary anymore?"

Many reading activities will be in the form of games. Concentration, Categories and others given in Chapter 8 can be devised to fit the particular lessons you are on. Children can be at a wide variety of reading levels and still play these games successfully. Some primaries are highly competent readers and could figure out how to pronounce *tabernacle* anywhere they see it. Others may know only that it is a long word and it matches with the other card that has a long word. Other children range somewhere between these extremes—some noticing more about the word's shape than just its length, some noticing that it starts with *t* or that it starts with *tab* and so forth.

So children can be learning at all levels. And while they may think of these as games, you can think of them as reading drills.

Some published lessons include the Bible story written in primary reading vocabulary. Since reading vocabulary, at this age, is not as large as the speaking or understanding vocabulary, these stories are not the main teaching of the Bible lesson. They are for reading instruction—instruction in reading Bible words, and eventually the Bible itself. A segment of the teaching period—perhaps five to seven minutes—should be used for such a reading lesson.

A normal reading lesson begins with an introduction of new words—*Elisha, widow* and other words which are necessary to the story, but which are not likely to be in the reading vocabulary of most of your children. Print the words on the chalkboard or flashcards, practice reading them together and individually. Find the words in the story. Have the children point to a word in their books. Check to see that everyone is pointing to the right one. How will they pronounce that word when they come to it in their reading?

After the introduction of new or difficult words, comes reading of the story. So that everyone has a chance to read, you can have partners read to each other, or everyone read silently. Only occasionally, for variety, will you or some children read while the class listens. A story written in play form, with speaking parts, is fun to do this way.

After reading the story, sometimes you can have a discussion or a check-up of the reading. How many wells did Isaac dig? Can you prove it from the story? Who can read to us what Pharaoh said?

If your lessons do not have primary stories, but only worksheets, you often can have reading lessons with those. Introduce new words and practice them before starting to work on the sheets. Sometimes go through the whole sheet together, reading questions and giving answers orally. Then take out pencils and have everyone work the sheet individually.

Some teachers are going to say, "That all works fine for large churches, but I have grades 1 to 3 all in one class." Those with mixed grades admittedly have a more difficult job, but not an impossible one. A word like tabernacle was not taught in any grade at public school. It is all yours to teach. This is the case with most of our specialized Bible words; many of the third graders need to learn them along with practically all first graders. So you can't drop your reading instruction just because you have a wider spead of abilities. Sometimes it works well to pair older children with younger children. The older child gets his reading practice by reading the story to the younger one, and the younger one at least hears the story. The older child can be given the assignment of teaching the younger one how to read one part of the story—perhaps one sentence. Or in some cases the younger child may learn how to spot a single key word—such as *God*—in the reading passage.

Even teachers with only one grade are not free from having a spread of abilities. One third grade class can have reading levels from early first grade to eighth or beyond. This is a fact of primary life we cannot escape. Actually, the better the teaching is the wider the spread will be. And your good teaching may only spread the abilities farther. Your goal can never be that everyone will learn the same things in the same amount, but you should aim to teach everyone something.

As you work at this you will gradually develop techniques for helping every child at his own level. Sometimes have both a silent reading group and an oral group. The silent readers can stay in their seats and the oral group meet in a corner to read the story aloud by turns. Sometimes everyone can read silently, except that you will listen to one child read. If this is an especially poor reader, you can read parts of the story to him and have him read small portions to you. When you find a system that works well for your class, you can use it routinely, only occasionally doing something else for variety.

So far we have considered reading Bible study materials which are written for primary children. Now what about the Bible itself? Should primary children be taught to read directly from the Bible? This question, unfortunately, is a highly emotional one with some people. Some teachers have turned to modern English translations so children can read earlier, and others feel such translations are not really the Bible. Some declare that if children were all put into Christian schools the reading problems would be at an end. There is a widespread belief that if something is good to learn, then learning it earlier is better yet.

But earlier is not always better. Sometimes it is inefficient; what you struggle to teach at age 6 may be taught easily at age 9. Sometimes it is inferior; what children may manage to recite by rote at age 6 can be an exciting insight at age 9. The "optimum age" principle should be applied to the matter of reading from the Bible. In other words, the real question is not how early we can manage it, but when the best or optimum time is.

In this, as in all skills, there is a wide variation among individual children. Some primaries will begin reading their Bibles without any nudging from a teacher. You may now and then have a pupil that you should encourage to read his Bible. But for the vast majority of primary children the optimum time is not yet.

That is, it is not yet time for totally independent reading and for using the Bible as the main study tool. But there are many "lead-in" activities that should happen during the primary years.

Here is an example of a lead-in activity. Have the children find Exodus in the table of contents in their Bibles. They can turn to Exodus by page number, and find where chapter 32 begins. At the beginning of that chapter they find the names *Moses* and *Aaron*, which you may have previously shown them on the chalkboard or flashcards. Then you explain to the children that that is where today's Bible story is found. Moses and Aaron are going to be in it. They can close their Bibles now and listen as you present the story of the golden calf by flannelgraph or reading or whatever method you choose.

Here is another example. During the reading time or worksheet time you can have your Bible open to the story of the day and have part of it marked for reading—a portion about one to five verses long. The better readers and others who wish to try can come to your Bible and read the verses.

Sometimes after you tell or read a story in its children's story form you might say, "If you read this story directly from the Bible this is how the last part (or some other part) would sound." Then read a key verse or two. Hearing the style of the sentences and the language used in Scripture will help children learn to read it.

Another idea, which many teachers use, is to help the

children locate a memory verse in their Bibles and read it from there or mark it for home study.

Let the children use the table of contents much of the time in finding books of the Bible. There is value in this, and this step should not be skipped over in a hurry to have the children memorize the books of the Bible. Since children *can* learn the books of the Bible by rote, many people have thought they *should* learn them—even as young as age 3. But here again the principle of optimum age should be observed. Is there real value in memorizing the books before children are able to read the Bible well enough to make use of this skill? Could the memorizing time at such young ages be put to better use memorizing something more worthwhile? The large majority of curriculum planners considering these questions have concluded that the optimum time for memorizing the books of the Bible is about fourth grade. With the recent increase in Christian schools, some will now say that children in such schools should memorize the books in third grade.

Before actually memorizing all the books, children should again have the experience of lead-ins. They should learn about Old and New Testaments and have practice finding this division in their Bibles. They should memorize Matthew, Mark, Luke, and John and know that these are where we can read about Jesus when He lived in the world. They can practice finding these, and can look for the name Jesus in them, or notice the red type in a red-letter edition. They can learn that the first book is Genesis and know that it tells about the beginning of things. They can learn that Psalms is close to the middle of their Bibles and they can try to find it without using the table of contents. They can learn a few other individual books as they study them in their lessons. They can become proficient in using the table of contents and in finding a particular chapter and verse once a book is located.

All these preliminary skills and knowledge are important steps that should not be skipped in a rush to have everyone recite the books of the Bible from memory. These skills make up what might be called a "readiness" program for using the Bible. The primary years should be devoted largely to these readiness skills and reading skills, and the actual memorizing of all the books should in most cases be reserved for about fourth grade.

READING CHECK

1. There are very few Bible stories that are appropriate for the younger primaries.   T   F

2. A good curriculum plan will teach doctrines in sequence — some at the primary level and some reserved for the older levels.   T   F

3. A good curriculum plan will teach doctrines in parallel fashion — teaching each at the primary level and expanding on each at the older levels.   T   F

4. Primary children should learn of God by learning His attributes.   T   F

5. Primary children should learn of God by learning things He said and did.   T   F

6. Death is one of the topics that should be reserved for children older than primary.   T   F

7. Concrete teaching means you must have specific examples instead of generalized principles.   T   F

8. According to the optimum time principle, we teach things as early as children can learn them.   T   F

9. If a teacher is not specifically trained in teaching reading he should not attempt this in Bible classes.   T   F

10. It usually is best not to require memory of the books of the Bible from all primary children.   T   F

4 Memorizing and Remembering

- *Do You Need a Theory?*
- *Faculty Theory*
- *Organization Theory*
- *What the Research Means to Us*
- *The Whole System of Memorizing*

Tom Sawyer was getting ready for Sunday school one morning, and part of the routine was his memory work. He had chosen five verses from the Sermon on the Mount "because he could find no verses that were shorter." Patient cousin Mary was helping him.

"Blessed are the —a—a—"

"Poor—"

"Yes—poor; blessed are the poor—a—a—"

"In spirit—"

"In spirit; blessed are the poor in spirit, for they—they—"

"*Theirs*—"

"For *theirs*. Blessed are the poor in spirit, for *theirs* is the kingdom of heaven. Blessed are they that mourn, for they—they—"

"Sh—"

"For they—a—"

"S, H, A—"

"For they S, H—oh, I don't know what it is!"

"Shall!"

"Oh, *shall*! for they shall—for they shall—a—a—shall mourn—a—a—blessed are they that shall—they that—a—a—they that shall mourn, for they shall—a—shall *what*? Why don't you tell me, Mary? What do you want to be so mean for?"

The story doesn't tell whether Tom remembered these particular verses long enough to earn his tickets, but he had his own system for collecting tickets. He traded "lickrish" and fishhooks and other valuables for them, and he eventually accumulated enough to be awarded a Bible. When a distinguished visitor was present, Tom chose that day to claim his prize. This led to great embarrassment for the superintendent but much hilarity for the readers.

That was Mark Twain's way of poking fun at the system of memorizing used in his day. And some features of that system are still widely used today, more than a century later—the feature, for instance, of leaving the memorizing up to the children and giving them no help in how to do it. Under this system the Marys make out all right but the Toms never do.

The feature of learning the verse at the last minute and remembering it only long enough to gain the points is still widely practiced. Some try to correct this weakness by having the children say a verse one week, and then say it again the next week to win their points. This may only result in two Tom and Mary Sunday morning episodes on the same verse, but still it is a slight improvement.

In Tom's day, people may not have thought about learning theories, but they operated pretty much by the "mind is a muscle" theory. If they could get children to use their minds, they would strengthen them. So they used what we call extrinsic motivation—motivators outside of the learning itself—tickets, points, prizes. Or at times they used punishment, in which case the children's motivation was to escape punishment.

Do You Need a Theory?

We no longer believe in the "mind is a muscle" theory, but our problem in memorizing is that we have no theory to replace it. Sometimes the visual aid idea is elevated to the status of a theory. We seem to think that if children see something, they are going to remember it longer than if they learn it some other way, so we try to visualize the memory verses as much as possible. This does work to some extent, but not for reasons of seeing; it works for reasons of associations and meanings, which will be explained more fully as we go along.

Yes, you do need a theory of memory. If you understand the deeper reasons why one method works better than another you can devise better plans for memorizing and for promoting the remembering of any teachings you wish.

The literature of research on memory is staggering in its bulk and complexity. It seems one needs to be a physiologist and chemist, as well as psychologist, to understand it. Memory, which once was considered the simplest aspect of our minds, and the easiest to research, is now revealing how very little we know about the incredible complexity that is the mind which God gave us. Though we know more than ever before, researchers realize, too, how great is our ignorance.

With all this help from research, we should be able to do a better job than Tom Sawyer's teachers. Here, we will distill from the research some things which are helpful to teachers. First, we will look at theories categorized into two major types—faculty theory and organization theory. Then we will describe a system for Scripture memory which draws upon insights from both kinds of theories.

Faculty Theory

This theory gets its name from the way it views memory as one "faculty" of the mind. That is, memory is seen as one factor distinct from other mental factors. A mathematical procedure called "factor analysis" enables researchers to sort out which mental abilities really are distinct from others, and which ones cluster together so that they should be given one name.

Some years ago Thurstone did this, measuring and factoring not physiological brain activity, but the output of the mind as subjects solved various test items. By this means he isolated quite a number of factors and identified seven groupings which he called "primary mental abilities." His seven abilities are: number ability, word fluency ability, verbal-meaning ability, associative-memory ability, reasoning ability, space ability, and perceptual-speed ability. To say that these abilities are distinct from one another, means that we will not necessarily find them high together or low together in any one pupil. A child who is high in number ability might be low in verbal-meaning ability and vice versa. A child who is high in both verbal-meaning ability and associative-memory ability will have an easier time memorizing Scripture than will his classmates who are lower in these abilities.

Thurstone developed an intelligence test which yields scores in these seven abilities. The scores totaled together yield an IQ score. Some people object to using IQ scores on the basis that they lump together diverse abilities and do not give us enough information about each child's specific strengths.

Guilford carried Thurstone's work still further. Not satisfied with the groupings of seven primary abilities, he studied about forty of the factors Thurstone isolated and conceived a new way to organize them. He developed a three-dimensional model of intellect. One dimension is the contents of thinking, the second is the operations, and the third is the products of thought. Diagramed, it looks like Figure 2.

If you look over the four kinds of contents to find the one which would include Scripture, you will locate "semantic," and in the operations you can locate "memory." On this cube, then, Scripture memory would be located on the pillar

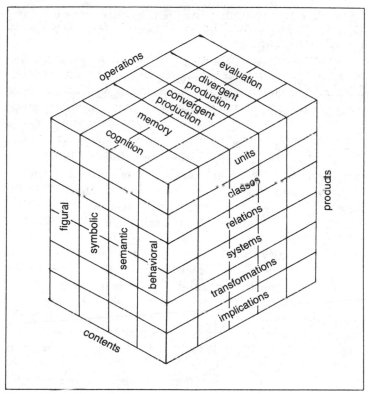

Diagram from "Three Faces of Intellect," by J. P. Guilford, *American Psychologist* 14 (1959, pp. 469-479).

Figure 2

that is found when you cross semantic content and the operation of memory. This pillar passes down through all six products. Some of the products are readily seen as part of Scripture memory. For instance, the units would be single words or thoughts of the passage, and relations would be relations between them, such as the order they come in, the way the meaning is related, and so forth. The more kinds of meaning we build in, the stronger will be the memory.

According to this theory there should be a mental factor

for each block in the cube. The memory slice alone contains twenty-four blocks, and about that many kinds of memory have been identified.

In order for the operation of memory to happen at all, one of the other operations must happen first. That is, the material to be remembered must first have been cognized or produced or evaluated by the mind. In other words, the mind can only remember those things which it has acted on in some way. This indicates to us that the crucial question is not whether the material enters the mind by the eyes, or ears, or fingers, or other means; the crucial question for memory is whether the mind acts upon the material. We must be sure that our children think about any content we want them to remember or to memorize. We will discuss this point in more detail further on.

Some faculty theorists study short-term and long-term memory. There is disagreement over whether these should be considered two different abilities. Some prefer to think of memory as a continuum ranging from short to long, with items placed anywhere on the scale. Others point to factor analysis research in which the two abilities factor out separately, and they point to physiological studies of the brain in which different capacities are used for short-term memory than for long-term memory. These theorists prefer to think of short-term and long-term memory as two separate abilities.

Either way, we find the concepts helpful. If it is a continuum, such as physical growth is, we can still use terms to talk about different ends of the scale. We talk about primary children or adolescents, and find these terms useful even though they are only points along the scale of growth. So, we can use the words short-term and long-term whether they are two separate abilities or points on a scale of ability.

This concept of short- and long-term memory is quite important for anyone working with Scripture memory. It is a great part of the difference between the Tom Sawyer method and the methods we should be using.

Research shows that short-term memory has a limited capacity. People can hold in this memory somewhere from five to nine items, or an average of seven. There are seven digits in most phone numbers, so if you are trying to hold each one separately until you dial, that would be about the limit. You might look at the phone book, get the numbers 675-8314 in mind, pick up the receiver, and then someone might say, "While you're talking to him, be sure to ask what time it starts and what we're supposed to bring to the dinner." After that interruption you are likely to have to look at the phone book again, as the new items drive the former items out of your head.

If you are in the habit of grouping numbers into "chunks," you can remember about seven of these chunks. Thus, the last four digits of the number above could be eighty-three fourteen. This makes it two items instead of four. And if the first three digits are the same as your own exchange they will already be in your long-term memory. In such a case, you might get through the interruption with the number still in your head. You would have two chunks of numbers and two brief messages to remember—four items all told. This is within the ordinary capacity of short-term memory.

In a primary class a teacher says, "His name is Zacharias. Try saying that name."

"Zacharias," the children chorus.

This technique serves to introduce the name and helps the children learn to pronounce it. But so far, it is only in their short-term memory. It will soon be driven out as the class moves on to other things.

How do you move items from short-term memory to long-term memory? We'll get to that after we take a look at another major view of memory.

Organization Theory

Have you ever gone back to visit some scene of your childhood and found it different from what you remembered? Have you read a favorite childhood book after you were grown and found it different from what you remembered? Many people have. What happens in these cases? Organization theory will help to explain it.

A little boy sat before a board that Piaget devised for memory experiments. The board was a square containing sixteen squares. On it were cards arranged with the largest across the top row, the next largest on the second row, and so on down to the smallest. This is called seriation according to size.

This particular board had another pattern, too. All the dark red cards were in the first column, those a little lighter were in the second column, and so on to the light pink in the fourth column. This is double seriation. The series is arranged by color if you look at the columns and it is arranged by size if you look at the rows.

This is rather complicated for many six-year-olds, but our boy with his own set of cards made an almost perfect copy of it. He made only one mistake in size. So his perception of the model was excellent. Now if memory depends on seeing, as the "visual aid theory" suggests, we could expect this boy to do quite well on an immediate memory test. But he didn't. When the model was removed and he was asked to make it again from his cards, he produced a jumble. Why?

Piaget knew that young children do not understand the double seriation format. So by this ingenious experiment he separated understanding from perception. He showed that memory is tied to understanding and not to perception. When this experiment is repeated with more children of different ages, the consistent result is that the children do as well as their mental development allows. Those who do not understand seriation perform as the boy already mentioned. Those who understand single seriation, remember the model in terms of one series—usually size. And those developed enough to understand double seriation can remember the model correctly.

The children in these experiments were tested for their

memory again a week later and six months later, and a surprising thing happened. Some children each time did better than on their first attempt. On these later attempts they did not see the model again and copy it again, they merely were asked to make it again as they remembered it, so what can these improvements be attributed to? They must be due to learning—to a better understanding of the scheme of seriation. For some children this may have come about through manipulating the model on the first memory test. Over the six month period any number of experiences could have brought about mental growth in this ability. Numerous other experiments on numerous other aspects of memory gave the same results, so that Piaget concludes that memory depends upon what he calls mental schemata.

Now back to your childhood memories—what accounts for certain things not being as you remembered them? When you were a child, your memories were formed according to your inner mental schemata and not according to your perception. When you go back now to the old homestead your schemata are not the same as they were years ago.

In many things you will have adjusted your memories over the years. For instance, the candy counter that loomed so high that you reached up to put your money on it, has become lower in your memory because intervening learning has told you how high candy counters are. Your schema now is adult and your memory adjusts accordingly. But with some memories you may have no opportunity for further learning. The family album may have no picture of the old house, so your memory has not become more accurate by learning, and thus the jolt when you see it again.

This view of memory shows it not as a distinctive faculty of intelligence, but rather as integrated with the total intellectual organization. Memory depends upon this organization.

Some forty years before Piaget's work on memory, a book by Bartlett called *Remembering* proposed this same view. Bartlett used the same term—schemata— to describe organizations within the mind. In some research which will interest us as Bible teachers who use stories a great deal, Bartlett studied subjects' memory for stories. He found that distortions which occurred were because of an effort after meaning. That is, if a person did not fully understand the story, he distorted it so it would fit into existing schemata in his mind. Piaget's more recent work is saying the same thing, although his experiments concern physical events rather than stories.

Bartlett's book, though remembered as an early classic on memory, was largely ignored while researchers all followed the faculty theory instead of his organization theory. But now with the high interest in Piaget's work we should see a renewed interest in research on the organization theory, and people may dust off Bartlett's book again.

What the Research Means to Us

If you stop at this point and ask yourself what these theories mean to your teaching, some principles are already quite obvious. For one, your children are not going to remember things they do not understand. Or they will distort them so they fit into their understanding. For another, your children do not remember things simply by seeing them; they must understand them and mentally act upon them. And for a third, learning something for immediate use results only in short-term memory.

These insights come both from faculty theory and from organization theory, as well as combinations of the two. The research of both types give us many other helps too.

The problem in memorizing is largely a problem of how to move material from short-term memory to long-term storage. Probably the most important element in this is time—time to rehearse mentally, time for repetition and practice, time for trying out the memory and relearning forgotten parts. Physiological studies, as well as psychological studies, show that time is needed for the memory trace to be consolidated. The time element can be used in the classroom in as simple a thing as learning one new word. "This man's name is Zacharias. I'm going to count to ten and then ask you to tell me his name." Then follows a silent ten seconds in which the children rehearse mentally and the name is set in memory more solidly than if it were repeated immediately after the teacher. A teacher won't always be wanting to count to ten during a class period, but many learning games and activities can be arranged to allow for mental rehearsal such as this, and other direct teaching situations can allow for thinking time.

Fast moving cartoons and TV commercials, and even the earlier days of Sesame Street, ignore this need for reflection in learning, and in effect teach children not to learn from the stimuli around them. Such "sensory overload" may be a cause of many perceptual learning difficulties which are in epidemic proportions today.

Another way to use time is in distributing the practice. It takes less total time to learn something if the learning is not done all at once, but is spaced out instead. If Tom had started earlier in the week he could have accomplished his task in less time. This effect has been shown in many studies, dating from the very earliest memory researches Various studies space the practice times from ten minutes apart to four days apart and find little difference in these time intervals; all are better than doing a similar amount of practice at one time.

Motivation is often considered important. From Tom Sawyer's tickets down to our Big Macs today, we feel we must work at motivation. But motivation seems not to have a direct effect on memory—only indirect, as it affects the time children spend on it and, perhaps, the level of concentration.

Besides time, the mental processing of material is also of major importance. This comes from both theories. Faculty theorists may speak of mental operations which must occur before there is anything for the memory to store. And organization theorists would speak of integrating the material to be remembered with the existing schemata of the intellect.

To process material, the mind must code it in some way. Usually we put things away in our minds in one of two ways—either as semantic (verbal) meaning, or as mental images. Images correspond to the figural content on Guilford's model of intellect. Some people do better at processing semantic meaning and others do better at processing images.

Imagery as a memory system has been taught from the time of the Greeks, down through Dale Carnegie, and more recently, Jerry Lucas. These imagery systems are forms of association learning. That is, you associate an image with an item you want to remember. This is one of the simplest, or lowest, forms of learning. That is, association is a simple kind of meaning; there is not a high level of meaningful relationships to understand, but only the "meaning" of association, and sometimes even these meanings are contrived. For instance, Carnegie taught people to memorize *run* for *one, zoo* for *two, tree* for *three*, and so forth. After memorizing the basic "pegs" a person can learn a list of other items by association with these. The first item can be associated with run in some sort of mental image; the second, with zoo; the the third, with tree, and so forth. For instance, if you are memorizing your grocery list you try to make a mental image of bread running, catsup behind bars in a zoo, and lettuce sitting in a tree. Then you just look through your images of run, zoo, and tree, and recall the other item in each image. It has been said that sillier images are better than more ordinary ones, but research has not borne this out.

We sometimes try to use this artificial kind of imagery when we visualize a verse word for word, using a bumblebee for *be*, an eye for *I*, and so forth. Since this technique calls upon only association learning—a low level—and since even the associations are contrived and meaningless to the context, we really should look for better ways to teach our verses.

Some people can easily produce vivid mental images, and they do exceedingly well with these association memory systems. They amaze the rest of us with their mental gymnastics and the prodigious amounts of memorizing they accomplish by this means.

At times we might wish we could improve our memories so that we could remember just everything. But we should be grateful that we cannot. Our thinking depends on being selective about what we perceive and what we make images of and store away in our memories.

A famous example of imagery gone wild is written up for us by the Russian psychologist, Luria (*The Mind of a Mnemonist*, New York: Basic Books, 1968). Luria's subject saw so many images that they crowded in upon him, interfering with his thinking. Where most of us try to learn how to remember, S. tried to learn how to forget. Everything turned to images in his mind. Even speech sounds emerged as lines, blurs and splashes. Sounds had form, color and taste. One time S. asked an ice cream vendor what flavor she had. The tone of her answer, "Fruit ice cream," conjured up an image of coals and black cinders coming out of her mouth so that S. was unable to buy any ice cream from her. S. said that other people think while they read, but he saw while he read. And the images piled up until they became positively distracting to any thinking. If an image provoked a thought, then that thought brought a new image to replace the one he started to think about, and in this way he got led far afield. He could not even recognize people's faces because he made such good images of every expression that he was confused by the constantly changing moods and expressions on faces.

This is image-making in the extreme. One of our great strengths in thinking is that we can ignore most things. We can abstract only certain features about a person's face and from these few features recognize it as the same face a moment later or days later. In a sentence we can abstract a certain thought or thoughts and dwell on those in our thinking. An image or feel or taste of every phrase, word, or letter sound does not intrude when we do not want it to.

Luria's subject illustrates for us one of the ways the mind codes information—one of four ways, according to Guilford's model. (See the four "contents" of thinking.) Children can be taught to make mental images of things they want to remember.

Children can also be taught to code things semantically. Classroom discussions where children talk and think about various Bible learnings help them code information semantically. In tests of picture memory, children are sometimes asked to think a sentence about a picture. This adds semantic meaning, and they remember the picture better than if they had merely seen it.

If a class is memorizing the Twenty-Third Psalm, they should at the same time be learning more about a shepherd, sheep, rod, staff and other items and ideas in the Psalm. All this learning adds semantic meaning and aids memory. All such learning also provides more associations for each item to be learned. And these are meaningful associations, not the contrived kind such as catsup in a zoo, or eye and I.

Most work in semantic meaning that we do with primary children will be to "expand" their meanings. For example, we show children a staff and then begin to expand on their meaning of it by teaching who used it, what he used it for, how it helped the sheep and so forth. Some semantic work can be called "condensing." When we ask, "What is a good title for this picture?" children do not begin naming all the details they see. Instead, they must lump them together in some kind of category and condense them into a title— "Shepherd Scene." Your lesson plan notes or speech notes are examples of condensing semantic meaning.

A remarkable example of condensed semantic coding is shown by Pastor Richard Wurmbrand, who spent fourteen years in communist jails in Romania. Three of those years were spent in solitary confinement underground. In an effort to keep his sanity, Wurmbrand composed a sermon each day and delivered it to himself. Then, in order to remember the sermons he put the main ideas into short rhymes. He memorized the rhymes and kept them in memory through repetition. Drugs from his oppressors erased the rhymes for a time, but they later came back. After his release he still remembered over 350 of the rhymes and he was able to reconstruct his sermons by means of them *(Sermons in Solitary Confinement*, London: Hodder and Stoughton, 1969).

This sort of condensing is what college students do when they memorize formulas and outlines and hope that at examination time they will be able to reconstruct whatever information is needed.

Both semantic coding and image (figural) coding enhance memory. At the present time there is no clear indication of which works best. Memory research involves memory for differing materials—sometimes pictures, sometimes word pairs, and others. They also involve various ages of children and adults. So in some situations imagery works slightly better and in some, semantic coding works slightly better. The one thing that is clear in all this research is that coding, or mental processing, of some kind is necessary to memory.

In summary, we have learned from the research that two important conditions for moving material into long-term memory are coding and time. Coding is the mind acting upon the material to translate it either into semantic meaning or figural meaning. Time is needed for the mind to do the coding. It is also needed for mental rehearsal, repetition and practice.

All these elements are worked into a system of Scripture memory which is described below.

The Whole System of Memorizing

Two second grade Sunday school classes learned Psalm 121 over a period of eight Sundays. One class practiced on the entire passage each week and the other class learned one verse of it each week. At the end of the time the first class could recite smoothly through the entire passage, and the second class needed prompting at the beginning of each verse. The two methods of memorizing used by these classes are known as the whole and the part methods.

The whole method helps semantic meaning, since relationships between the parts become more evident when the material is practiced as a whole. It also makes better use of time; spacing, repetition and practice are arranged more efficiently. All these features fit with the general memory research we have been looking at.

In addition to all these supports, we have specific research on memorizing literary passages. Experimental studies comparing the whole and the part methods of memorizing literary passages began as early as 1900. At that time a series of experiments was made using both adults and children. In every experiment in the series the whole method resulted in less time needed for learning. Since these early studies, the results have been corroborated many times by other researchers.

Some of the later researches began pointing out other advantages for the whole system in addition to efficiency. These included the facts that when associations were made they remained; everything was always in the same place; the interrelationships of parts and the organization of the whole became clearer. Thus there was a deeper understanding of the poem or prose passage, and what was memorized lasted longer. So this early research shows three major advantages for the whole system of memorizing: 1) greater efficiency, 2) more meaning, and 3) longer retention.

Why has this early research been so largely ignored and our Christian education efforts in memorizing commonly taken a different path? There probably is no single answer to this question, but possible answers may lie in several problems that people meet in implementing this system.

One of the problems is to find a proper size unit to learn. The unit should be as large as the learner or learners can handle meaningfully. This varies with the age and intelligence of the learners. And it also varies with their exposure to and familiarity with the type of material. As a person becomes more familiar with the style of writing, the kind of language, the concepts, and other characteristics of the writing, memorizing becomes easier. The first chapter one learns from Paul's letters will take longer than the second. Children who are not used to the vocabulary and sentence construction of Bible verses will take longer to memorize a verse than will children who have had much exposure to this language. For some, a unit should consist of a full chapter or a selected portion of a chapter, or for younger memorizers it may be a single verse. The size of the unit can vary according to the content of the passage, the age and ambition of the memorizer, the amount of time available, and other factors.

Another problem to overcome in using the whole memory system is the resistance that appears in the early stages of the process. When nothing seems actually memorized after a time of working on a passage, doubts set in about the efficacy of memorizing this way. Many teachers on the first day would rather hear the children recite, "The Lord is my shepherd; I shall not want." This tangible evidence of learning may be more satisfying to the teacher, and she reasons that she can tack on verse 2 at the next session and continue working on parts in this way until the whole psalm is learned. This temptation to memorize just one part happens both when it is one person memorizing by himself and when it is a teacher helping children to memorize.

If you are the teacher, you need not worry about your children losing their motivation. Children's motivation is significantly affected only if they are left to do the memorizing entirely on their own. But with the whole method, they should not be left on their own because children need considerable training and experience in the method before they can use it by themselves. It works better if you take class time and build the memorizing into your lesson plans. You can help the children by a variety of classroom procedures. These are usually motivating in themselves and the child is not disturbed if he leaves class the first day and cannot quote the first verse of a passage the class is starting to learn. It is usually only the teacher who is disturbed by this. Those who persevere in the method in spite of the seeming slow start are often greatly surprised by the results.

Still another problem with the whole method concerns the hard and easy parts. After working for a time on a passage, the easy parts will already be learned and some hard parts will remain unlearned. This problem can be solved by departing at times from the whole method and putting extra effort on the hard parts. This departure from a strictly whole method is incorporated in the procedure recommended below.

If we take into account research on processing, semantic coding, imagery, associations, time factors, distribution of practice, and other topics discussed in this chapter, the whole method can be outlined as a four-step procedure as follows.

1. Become familiar with the whole unit.
2. Review the whole unit many times with concentration and with different approaches or contexts.
3. Put extra work on the difficult parts, if necessary.
4. Overlearn.

Be sure to do a good job of Steps 1 and 2 before beginning Step 3. In actual practice this step overlaps the others. That is, all hard parts should not be learned at once, but they should be attacked one at a time, and all the while work should continue on the whole. But this work on parts is placed at Step 3 in the sequence to indicate that it should not start too soon. The learning must be well along before it even becomes clear which parts are going to be the hard ones.

Using this basic sequence, an infinite number of teaching-learning plans can be devised. A very young child who is just learning to talk can be taught passages as long as the Twenty-Third Psalm or even longer. To do this the child's mother or "teacher" begins by saying a short phrase and the child repeats it after him. Then the teacher says the next phrase and the child repeats it. They continue in this way through the whole psalm. The procedure is repeated daily, and the teacher gradually increases the length of the phrases. Later she just starts the phrases and lets the child finish them himself when he can. At this point her help diminishes with each repetition of the psalm and the child says more of it on his own and eventually he says the entire psalm with no help at all.

A child who has learned the psalm in this way will see it as one piece. He will recite straight through it as most children recite through the alphabet, without stopping at the end of a verse and wondering which verse comes next. With such a young child there is naturally less reliance on meaning than there is with older children.

With primary children you can use a variety of methods to familiarize them with the memory passage and to give practice in Steps 1 and 2 of the memory process. The children can read the passage, answer questions about it, discuss difficult parts, have relays to put things in order, play various other games with it. When the passage is learned, the games and drills should continue for a time so that overlearning can take place. And then, ideally, there should be an occasional review of the passage. Reviews should be spaced closer together at the first and then gradually spaced farther and farther apart. When a passage has been well learned and overlearned, reviewing it just once or twice a year during the school years will serve to make it a permanent part of a student's mental equipment.

Following is a sample set of lesson plans for helping primary children to memorize Psalm 23. You will notice in this that meaning is not taught all at once, but spaced throughout. Review of meaning, just as review of the words, follows the principles of repetition and spaced practice. The variety of games and procedures heightens concentration.

Each repetition is not exactly the same and the newness of standing on one foot, closing eyes, looking for pronouns, and so forth gives the children always something to concentrate on.

You will notice, also, the four steps of the procedure. They all overlap to some extent. Step 1, familiarizing, begins in Lesson 1 and continues until about Lesson 6. Step 2, practicing the whole, begins in Lesson 3 and continues through all the lessons. It should even extend into any later overlearning and review of this psalm. Step 3, work on hard parts, is mostly in Lessons 9 and 10. It could extend longer, if necessary. Step 4, overlearning, may begin at about Lesson 8 for some pupils and extend through Lesson 12 and any further reviews.

Lesson 1. Look at and talk about various sheep and shepherd pictures or, if you have it, a specially prepared picture set for Psalm 23. As you talk use the words *still waters, valley, rod, staff, shepherd, oil*, and others which may appear in the pictures. Read through the entire psalm from a large chart or from the picture set.

Lesson 2. Read the psalm phrase by phrase and have the children repeat carefully after you. Correct any mispronunciations; insist on accuracy. Review about two of the pictures by having children tell what they know about them. Teach the meaning of one or two phrases such as "preparest a table" or "cup runneth over."

Lesson 3. Read through the psalm together. If you have a picture set, several children will each want a chance to turn the pages and you may get the class to read the psalm several times. Or the children can read the psalm standing on one foot, standing behind their chairs, sitting cross-legged, etc. Let them think of other ways to read it. Talk about enemies. Do the sheep have enemies? Do the children have enemies or other things to be afraid of? What does the shepherd do about it?

Lesson 4. Explain that *restoreth* means *make new again*. Illustrate with a story of a sick sheep that is now well again because the shepherd took good care of it. Read the psalm together several times using your chart or picture set. Ask who can point to a part that will be good to think about when they are afraid. Have each child who chooses a part try to tell why he chose it.

Lesson 5. Read through the psalm together. See who remembers what *restoreth* means. Teach one or two other difficult words. Have all the children close their eyes and see if they can finish each phrase of the psalm after you start each one. Proceed through the entire psalm in this way.

Lesson 6. Have the children look through the psalm and find four words that name themselves. (I, my, me, mine.) List these words on a chalkboard as the children find them. Ask the children to say or read the psalm together, and every time they come to one of the four words say it much louder. Do this more than once. Have identical sets of the psalm cut into several pieces. Form teams and see which can first assemble a set in order. Scramble the pieces and try this again and perhaps a third time. Let individual children race while the others look on.

Lesson 7. Have the children find all the words that refer to God. (Lord, shepherd, He, his, thou, thy.) Read through the psalm emphasizing all those words. This may be difficult to do; try marking the words and reading the psalm again. See who remembers the meaning of the words you taught in Lesson 5. If the children want to do relays again, as in Lesson 6, let them.

Lesson 8. Read or say the psalm together. Have a set of cards with simple pictures which can illustrate the psalm. (These may be Jesus, pasture, still water, path, valley, rod, staff, table, horn of oil, cup, "House of the Lord.") Pass out the cards to the children. Ask for whoever thinks he has the first picture to come up and place it on the flannelboard (or chalk ledge, or floor). Then the one who thinks he has the next picture can come, etc. The children who are watching are to raise their hands any time they see something they think should be changed. When you call on them they may make the changes. Continue until everyone agrees that the pictures are in correct order. Say the psalm together as you point to each picture in turn.

Lesson 9. Have the children find Psalm 23 in their Bibles. Ask them each to select the verse that is hardest for them to say. Let each child work alone or with a partner, as he prefers, and study his verse. He should try to say it with no errors. After sufficient study time repeat the entire psalm together.

Lesson 10. Have the children all get partners and see if they remember the verses they studied last week. Those who make errors should study the same verse this week. Others should select a different verse to study this week. After a limited time, repeat the entire psalm together. If possible, arrange an audience, such as parents or another class, for the children to recite the psalm to. Announce this today so the children can be anticipating it.

Lesson 11. Use the pictures from Lesson 8 and show them one at a time in scrambled order and have the class say a part of the psalm that goes with each picture. Then let one or more of the children put the pictures in order. Repeat the entire psalm together, looking at the pictures. Scramble the pictures again and let different children put them in order. Say the psalm again. Remind the children of their public recitation. Does anyone want to do extra study at home?

Lesson 12. Pretend there is an audience and practice reciting for them. Speak together. Use good expression. Try it several times. Is everyone ready for the public recitation?

(Adapted from Accent Bible Curriculum.)

READING CHECK

1. The mind is like a muscle; it needs exercise to become strong.   T   F

2. In faculty theory, memory is viewed as a distinctive mental ability.   T   F

3. According to organization theory, if your children see something they will remember it.   T   F

4. According to organization theory, your children must fit new learning into their existing understandings before they can remember it.   T   F

5. If children explain to you a picture about still waters, they are coding the meaning semantically.   T   F

6. If children make a mental picture of Jesus dressed as a shepherd, they are coding meaning in an image.   T   F

7. Imagery is superior to other forms of coding.   T   F

8. At primary age it is best to send a memory verse home and let each child learn it in his own way.   T   F

9. After a Scripture passage is learned, it should be reviewed every day.   T   F

10. The whole method of memory is superior to the part method.   T   F

Answers: 1—F, 2—T, 3—F, 4—T, 5—T, 6—T, 7—F, 8—F, 9—F, 10—T.

5   Curriculum

- *Begin with Values*
- *Organization of Content*
- *Look at the Important Things*

In chosing curriculum materials it is helpful to understand something of how they are—or should be—developed. The starting place is to decide what we want to teach. This, in essence, is deciding what we value.

The free public school movement in America was motivated largely by early Americans' belief in democracy. They *valued* democracy. In the democracy, they reasoned, all citizens needed to know how government works; therefore they needed to learn such things as history, government, and reading. Also in the democracy each person was valued for himself, so he needed opportunity to learn the things that could enrich his life. This contrasts with, for instance, feudal times where the apprentice learned what would profit his master.

Ancient Jewish education, such as Paul had, was centered around the Scriptures. Boys learned to read so they could read the Scriptures. Christian schools throughout the Christian era have been started for the same purpose.

This is over-simplified, of course, as all other intellectual pursuits, as well as artistic and physical pursuits, have also been a part of schooling down through the ages. But the point is that schooling reflects what the society values. The Christian community embedded within secular society has its own set of values, and the growing Christian school movement in America is an indication of the increasing conflict between its values and that of the secular society around it.

A full-orbed Christian education encompasses all of learning, using the Biblical view in even the so-called secular subjects. But in this book we are using the term "Christian education" in a narrower sense to refer to the child's learning of Christianity.

Begin with Values

Now, the starting point for curriculum is to determine what we value. It is fashionable today to state this in the form of an objective. In other words, we decide what we hope to accomplish, and make this statement of purpose or objective. But behind the objective is our value system.

In a moment we will look at an example of such a statement from a denominational board of education, but first let's have a story of vitamins. What does that have to do with curriculum? Well, hang on. You just might see a connection.

Early in the century, with beriberi outbreaks, it became obvious that brown rice had something white rice was lacking. Dr. Casimir Funk, a Pole in England, obtained almost a ton of rice. He spent four months removing the polishings, then removing this part and that part until he was down to almost a pure chemical—six ounces of thiamin, or Vitamin B1. This was the first vitamin discovered. It now sells for about $5000 a pound in pill bottles, but is still obtainable in whole grains and meat for considerably less than that.

Vitamin B1 is now often added to white rice, white flour and other products. When man in his wisdom attacks the grain God has given, he emasculates it of about twenty-four known nutrients and, no doubt, some unknown ones too. Then he mixes back in about six weaker, synthetic nutrients.

Now back to curriculum. Watch what happens when

man processes God's revelation through the curriculum mill. It is hard work. Boards and committees everywhere have sweated over their guiding statements of purpose, or objective. They want them inclusive but brief, broad but specific, accurate but clear. Here is one example.

The objective of the church as manifested through its educational ministry is that all persons be aware of and grow in their understanding of God, especially of his redeeming love as revealed in Jesus Christ, and that they respond in faith and love—to the end that they may know who they are and what their human situation means, increasingly identify themselves as sons of God and members of the Christian community, live in the spirit of God in every relationship, fulfill their common discipleship in the world, and abide in the Christian hope.

That mouthful is typical of numerous such efforts. It may sound quite comprehensive and good upon first reading. Once the statement is made, the education board proceeds to delineate the scope of the curriculum. In this case the board listed three dimensions of reality—the divine, the human, and the natural. Sounds comprehensive. But is it? Does this include the Satanic—sin and evil?

The three dimensions are said to be aspects of man's experience "in the whole field of relationships." The idea of man's relationships is mentioned in the original objective, and now it is singled out as the entire scope. "Therefore," the curriculum design book says, "the elements of the scope . . . are identified as these three":

The Christian experience of man under God—
    the divine reality in light of the gospel

The Christian experience of man's relation to man—
    the human dimension of reality in light of the gospel

The Christian experience of man within the world—
the natural dimension of reality in light of the gospel

This little maneuver has resulted in considerable distilling of the original three dimensions. Even if the divine, the human and the natural are the total of reality—and it is not clear that they are—this further statement has not included all the possibilities for study. For one thing, it focuses only on relationships between elements and never on the elements themselves. For another, it starts with man and lists his relationships only. Notice that relationships between the divine and the natural are not even included. The world is groaning under the curse, and looking for its deliverance by God. This relationship between the divine and the natural has, perhaps unwittingly, been distilled out of this curriculum. The value placed on man and his relationships has slanted the curriculum in a particular direction.

After the three elements, this committee identified five areas. The areas act as cross sections. Each element is studied as it falls on each of the cross sections. Further distillation. By continued refinement of this type a curriculum committee can eventually find a few vitamins and serve up their nutritious concoction to all the children in their care.

Curriculum committees are wrestling with an old, old problem. Man has always tried to organize his knowledge in one way or another. Structure of some kind helps his thinking along. Christian education is struggling for a structure these days.

One committee decided it could all be summed up in the three ideas of Christ, the Bible, and the Church. Spend one year studying each topic, then rotate back through the topics again. With high hopes the program was instituted, but it floundered before the second cycle.

The more liberal denominations got into this serious curriculum business first. They attacked it like educational philosophers. Then the more conservative organizations moved into the field. Some of them by-passed philosophy and latched onto the then-popular psychological theories. In effect, they made psychology their philosophy. If Abraham Maslow said people have such and such needs, then our job was to meet those needs. If Erik Erikson said people pass through such and such stages (sometimes called crises), then we should find Bible portions to help them through each crisis. If Jean Piaget said children pass through such and such stages in their mental development, then we need to be on the spot helping them onto the next stages. If Robert Havighurst said his list of developmental tasks describes the social growth of people, then we need to see how the Bible applies to each task.

Man's philosophy has never answered man's deepest questions, so it has failed as a foundation for Christian education curriculum. Man's psychology is failing too. It is a help in many aspects of Christian education, but as a basis, or organizing principle, for curriculum it will inevitably be shown to be only as strong or as weak as the amount of Biblical truth in the theories being used.

So if the basis of a curriculum plan is not to be found in philosophy or psychology, where is it found? The obvious answer is that we find it in God's revelation to man—the Bible. This is the whole bread. Instead of trying to extract vitamins from it according to our psychological or philosophical beliefs, we can use the bread itself as the basis for our curriculum plans. When we do this many of the diseases and deficiencies will never happen and we will not have to worry so much about meeting them.

A good many Christian teachers, of course, have never left the whole bread of God's Word. But some may be feeling guilty because of all the psychological talk around them of meeting the self-esteem need or the identity crisis or of using only measurable behavioral objectives. Curriculum materials, too, sometimes are actually organized around Bible content but dressed in the current psychological jargon. These fashionable ideas are much talked about but not so often actually practiced.

The natural inclination of Christians is to value the Bible, and most want a curriculum that will feed this whole bread to their children. They do not want to substitute the "vain philosophies" of men for the revelation that God Himself has given. Thus the major part of Christian education and the basis of all Christian education is the Bible itself. If churches add on missionary education, music education, study of cults, and other such topics, it is because these grow out of the Bible teachings. The Bible is at the center and learning expands outward.

This is God-centered. It is from God to man. It is God teaching man. It moves in the opposite direction from man-centered education, in which humanists try to identify the "diseases" of man, and curriculum planners distill some Bible vitamins to treat the diseases.

So when you are choosing curriculum materials, the most important thing to know about a curriculum is its value basis. Does it value the Bible enough to frankly base its plan upon Bible content? And does it use psychological knowledge only secondarily to help gear its lessons to the interests and abilities of the various age groups? Or does it put modern psychological beliefs (or philosophical statements) at the base and pick and choose Bible content accordingly?

The problem is not quite as simple as deciding whether a curriculum is Bible-centered or man-centered. Two curriculums may claim to be based on the Bible without too many psychological gimmicks, but their doctrinal interpretations of the Bible could differ. If you are not yet able to judge in doctrinal matters, then you need the help of your pastor or perhaps another staff member. As you teach the sound doctrine your pastor chooses, you will eventually become a good judge yourself of doctrinal matters found in curriculum materials.

The first step in curriculum planning, then, is to decide on content. In curriculum jargon this is called "scope." The content is inevitably based on values. As a curriculum user you need a close match between your own values and those of the developers of the curriculum.

Organization of Content

Once the content is chosen, the next step is to organize it in some systematic and meaningful way. Curriculum people have a jargon for this too. The word is "sequence."

Our minds need some sort of structure and sequence. We like to know where to put things and how to relate them to other things. Order in our houses keeps them from resembling garbage dumps. Order in our minds makes them livable.

When Jesus taught on the Emmaus road He *began* at Moses and all the prophets, and He expounded unto them in all the *Scriptures concerning Himself* (Luke 24:25-27). Here is both an order and an organizing theme.

After the resurrection Jesus taught His disciples for forty days about "the kingdom of God" (Acts 1:3). Peter's sermon in Acts 2 connects the prophecies of Joel and David with the current events. Stephen's sermon in Acts 7 begins with Abraham and recounts the story of the Israelites' relationship with God. Paul fed the Corinthians first with milk, looking forward to the time when they could take meat.

Organization is unavoidable. That's what sequence in curriculum is all about. To simplify the discussion here we will consider only the basic Bible education. That is, we will not include such things as a church's education concerning its own missionary program. For a basic Bible education, churches usually look to publishers, and the discussion here is to help you evaluate the materials you are using or any you may wish to use.

What should a primary sequence be? This is a difficult question for curriculum developers to wrestle with. One of the earliest, and still common, decisions was to start with Genesis and go through the Bible. Some juggling was usually imposed on this order so as not to stay in the Old

Testament too long at one time, and so as to be in season at Easter and Christmas.

At first look this may seem the ideal solution. It looks complete, orderly, and easy to understand. But with more thought, problems emerge. The biggest problem is that it simply is impossible to study through the Bible with primaries. Some stories and Scripture passages will be selected and others counted out. Some reasons for this were enumerated in the first section of Chapter 3. There are other reasons, too, including such mechanical ones as time limitations.

Imagine that you have the job of starting through the Bible to list stories for a chronological primary curriculum. You begin with stories of creation, of Adam and Eve, and of Cain killing Abel, unless you decide that is too violent for young children. Even if you leave the first murder on your list it will not be long before you come to something that seems too gruesome or too sex-oriented so that you decide to skip it. Throughout your listing your own values will be expressed in what you select and what you leave out. This is inevitable. So it is in chronological curriculum.

The value of chronological study of the Bible is not the only one to consider. There are also the values hidden in the selection processes. And these values can slant the curriculum in one direction or another. For instance, you could choose only stories which show God's loving care, and omit stories which show His hatred for and judgment on sin (which really is also part of the holiness and glory of God). In this way you would present a one-sided view of God. Some years ago this approach fit with the popular psychology that children would naturally bloom as good little flowers. There was no evil in them and we should not teach them about evil or that God hates it and judges it. So a curriculum which claims merely to go through the Bible actually could be guided by psychological values which you may or may not agree with. In selecting, you need to look for such values which may be stated or which may have crept in unaware and be unstated.

Still another problem with chronological organization for primaries is that of building larger meanings. An important curriculum principle is that content should be organized in a meaningful way. Small learnings should build up to "big ideas." Beginning with your imaginary list of stories that began with creation and proceeded through the Bible, how would you organize into meaningful units? What are the big ideas you would build toward? The obvious ideas are those related to historical chronology—the history of the early world, God's unfolding plan of redemption, the history of God's chosen people, and so forth. But these historical meanings are a kind that primary children are not yet able to handle. Children who have only lived six or seven years do not understand the passing of generations. They simply do not have the time concepts needed for a good understanding of history. But when you have chosen your stories on the basis of their historical order you have no other logical themes to put upon them. Anything you try will be strained. So you can organize units around some strained themes, or you can forget big ideas altogether and just go along lesson by lesson learning whatever comes up each time. But, in giving up big ideas, you lose a lot of teaching power.

These are some of the problems inherent in a chronological curriculum for primaries. It is an uphill battle for lesson planners.

The other obvious arrangement is to use topics of some kind. And this raises the questions: Where will we get the topics? and What authority or criteria will validate these topics to us as being the best ones? We are right back again to the beginning question of values. If we use topics such as "You Are Special" we value psychology. We may try to list topics from the Bible itself and find things like friendliness, hospitality, courage, love, faith. But we would have to ask how we know the list is a complete or balanced view of the Bible we are trying to teach. What criteria, or values, are behind our selection?

Some widely-used topics are biographical. In these, primary children learn about Abraham's life or David's life, for example. This has some features of chronological organization, and it is an introduction for children into historical order in a way that is quite meaningful to them. While they may understand very little of Abraham's or David's place in the history of Israel or in God's plan of redemption or any other larger view, they can do quite well in learning about the life of one man and of gaining lessons for living from it.

But the whole Bible, or a balanced view of the Bible, cannot be taught biographically. This organization can be only a part of what we do at primary level.

A most promising set of topics is theological. If we are going to teach the Bible in a topical way, what better place to get our topics than from the experts in Bible study—the theologians? A theological list comes out of the Bible, rather than being exterior to it as with the psychological approaches. Since it comes out of the Bible, and since it is developed by Bible scholars, it has perhaps the best claim to comprehensiveness that we can attain.

A unit in this kind of curriculum might be diagramed with a circle at the center. Consider, for instance, a subunit on the doctrines of God in which you are teaching that God is all-powerful. (See Figure 3.)

Your central idea—that God is omnipotent—is first translated from an adjective to a verb and now reads, "God is over all things." This verb form is more understandable to primary children. Around this theme you organize your lessons. Each one is a story or incident which concretely demonstrates God's power. You may have subunits as you go along—such as "God has power over nature." "God has power over nations," and others. Everything contributes to the big idea you are teaching.

Missionaries in training are now being taught this circular, unitary, arrangement for teaching and for preaching to peoples who have little academic background. Our primary children also have limited academic backgrounds and

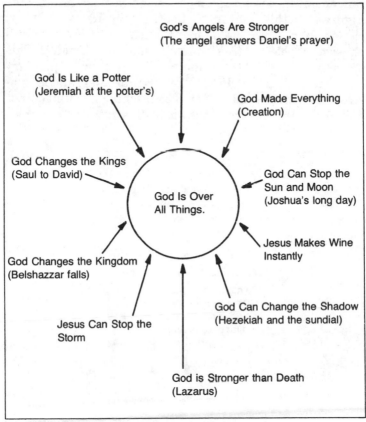

Figure 3   (From Accent Primary Curriculum)

they have concrete ways of thinking. One missionary re-
ports, "One of the things we learned in twenty years of
trying to teach our people is that they can understand concrete things. We give them the book of Mark instead of the
book of John." Like little children in our civilization, they
must start with stories as stories. And if the missionaries
start out this way the people may some day graduate to the
book of John.

Contrast this circular arrangement with the linear arrangement that is used in a chronological curriculum. (See Figure 4.) In this diagram we list the story first, since it was chosen first. Then one or more possible teachings to emphasize are selected from the story and listed under it. This story-teaching construction is inherent in a primary chronological curriculum. The circular diagram is constructed in the opposite order. The teaching is selected first, and stories are selected as they help illustrate the teaching.

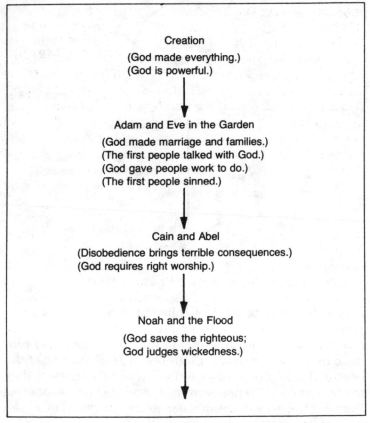

Creation
(God made everything.)
(God is powerful.)

Adam and Eve in the Garden

(God made marriage and families.)
(The first people talked with God.)
(God gave people work to do.)
(The first people sinned.)

Cain and Abel

(Disobedience brings terrible consequences.)
(God requires right worship.)

Noah and the Flood

(God saves the righteous;
God judges wickedness.)

Figure 4

When curriculum is built around big ideas, the learning is more meaningful at all levels. Even the "little ideas" mean more and are remembered better. This principle is explained in more detail in the chapter on memorizing and remembering. Meaningfulness also has a great deal to do with setting children up for future learning. A child with good doctrinal background given concretely at primary level will have little difficulty at teen level with deeper, more abstract doctrinal studies. He already has a place in his mental schemata for fitting these learnings.

Look at the Important Things

To look backward, we have considered in these sections two basic curriculum procedures. First, the content must be chosen, and everyone—user and developer alike—should be aware of the values that inevitably play a part here. Next, the content must be organized. This is a complicated process that involves knowing the Bible and the general abilities of children. It uses curriculum principles and learning theory. Usually a team of people are involved in this process.

The third big step in developing a curriculum is to plan the lessons. Again, this takes knowledge of teaching and learning, as well as writing, art, and other skills if the curriculum is to be published for others to use. Denominational headquarters and independent publishing houses have spent years of time and considerable sums of money to do this work for your church or school or club.

If you are on a selection committee, people may be saying, "Look at the bright color on these visuals," or "Look at this cartoon art." You may have a checklist which asks you to mark whether the lessons have behavioral objectives. (It may not even ask about the *content* of the objective, simply whether it is stated in behavioral terms!)

When the committee is taken up with trivial matters you can be the one to raise the big questions. What does this material teach? What values are behind the selection of content? How is the content organized? Does it build toward big ideas? What are they?

This work is not as easy as looking at color, but it's closer to what curriculum selection committees should be doing. And if you do it, both you and your children will be the winners.

READING CHECK

1. The starting point for curriculum planning is with values.   T   F

2. One of the earliest organizations of primary Bible curriculum was chronological.   T   F

3. One of the best organizations of primary Bible curriculum is chronological.   T   F

4. A good organization for primary curriculum is topical. T   F

5. A major concern in selecting curriculum is that it teaches what the church wants to teach.   T   F

6   *Teaching with Stories*

- *The Value of Stories*
- *Presenting Stories*
- *Preteaching*
- *Follow-Up*

The Value of Stories

God is the first and greatest storyteller. He opens His Book with the story of creation. Men will never plumb the depths of that story. God tells us things that Adam and Eve did, and even words that they spoke. No philosopher He, with wordy treatises on how evil came into the world. He simply tells the story of what happened.

God's Book doesn't sound like a history text telling us about a nomadic tribe that grew in numbers and power and on such-and-such a date overcame some other tribes. Not at all. Through stories we know the man Abraham—loving his beautiful wife, generous toward his nephew, courageously rescuing Lot, talking with angels and God. We know Isaac—not as adventurous as either his father or his sons. We know the other patriarchs and Noah and Moses.

Even when it came time to give the law, this didn't emerge as a dull report from a committee room. No, it thundered from the mountaintop with fire and smoke. The story has thundered round the world and through the ages.

God is the original Storyteller. Literature, from ancient

times, has emulated the first stories, but never equals them.

Teaching with stories is more like feeding whole-grain bread than synthetic vitamins. Stories teach on all levels and may be most powerful of all at the children's level. Try thinking back to your own experience with the story of Cinderella. You might have felt sad for Cinderella in rags working by the fire. You might have felt hatred or disgust for the step-mother and the sisters. Excitement and hope entered, and pleasure in the beauty of Cinderella's magical clothes, and satisfaction at the outcome of the story. You identified according to your own situation in life. Various psychological needs and mental levels affect the way children see a story, and it is full of human meaning for them.

Now you are an adult and you can be more analytical about it. You can say that's just a fairy tale with a happy ending. You might see it as wish-fulfillment of some early story writer. Or you might think of economics—that the "rags to riches" idea doesn't often happen in real life; you have to work hard if you want to get ahead in the world.

Or you might think along literary lines and find a spiritual analogy. The bride is clothed in garments not her own and the king's son comes to claim her for himself. How like Christ and His bride! And this may well be the origin of the story idea. There have been found 345 versions of this tale from all parts of the world. Some, such as the Irish and the Russian versions, have the girl going off to mass rather than to a ball. In the Irish version, finding the bride is not yet the happy ending. The prince still has to fight hard for her, and blood is shed before they can live peacefully together. Here is more material for analogy with the gospel story. Christ is the original Hero, just as God is the original Storyteller.

Now, as an adult you can do all this analyzing of the Cinderella story. But is there anything like the power the story had when you were a child—especially if you were a girl and pictured yourself with a slim waist and long hair in the most beautiful dress imaginable, and being sought by

The Hero?

If you happen not to have been brought up on Cinderella you will have to make up your own illustration from something else that was important in your childhood—the flag waving at the head of a parade, the wind blowing across a golden field of wheat, the whole congregation singing "We're marching to Zion." This emotion, human meaning—whatever it is—never comes again with the same power it did in childhood. We should give our young children rich experiences of Bible stories. The nourishment will far outlast much of our other teaching.

In Bible stories there often is a polarization. Two of Aaron's sons offered strange fire and died. Two did not, and they lived. In the congregation of Israel some followed rebellious Korah and some did not. The earth opened to swallow the "bad guys," while the "good guys" lived. God helped one side win the battles. He stopped the sun, or parted the waters, or dropped the hailstones. And the other side met destruction.

With opposites such as these, young children can easily understand the differences. Ambiguities and complexities of life can come at a later time in the child's growing, but first he needs to see clearly the choice of being on God's side or not. According to psychiatrist Bettelheim, the child does not ask, "Do I want to be good?" but he asks, "Who do I want to be like?" (*The Uses of Enchantment*, New York: Knopf, 1976, p. 10.) He does this by identifying with the hero of the stories. He wants to be David and not Goliath, Noah and not someone outside the ark. The definitiveness of the fates of these story characters provides clarity for the child. With story elements he begins sorting out life and building meaning for himself.

There is not only polarization of good and evil—of God's side and the other side. Stories have, also, other realities. Here the child meets death and the struggles of life. He learns to handle these in his thinking and his feelings. Many things that we wouldn't want him to learn by experience, he can learn through stories. Stories help him grow.

Stories provide more "models" than we could ever give the child in life. Life moves slowly and it limits what a child can learn from live models. Only in reading and hearing of other completed lives can a child gain so much experience in so short a time.

If we believed more in the whole-grain bread of the stories, perhaps we would not feel so compelled to scratch out vitamins for the child. When Daniel's three friends refuse to bow to the statue, does the story really need this? "Now boys and girls we have idols too. They may not be gold statues, but other things in our lives can be idols if they become too important to us. And do you see what these three friends did? They did not bow down." Or when David cuts off a piece of Saul's robe should we insert our sermon? "Now you see, boys and girls, David could have killed his enemy, but he didn't. God wants us to love our enemies"?

A sermon is usually strengthened by stories in it, but a story is not strengthened by sermons in it. We can save our sermonizing for later in the lesson. In dispensing vitamins we might try to give out vitamin B1 while one child may desperately need B6, and another, Vitamin C. Some may have no use for B1 now, but if it's stored away in its easily remembered story form it will be available for use when needed.

This is what Bettelheim found in his study of children and the old tales. He states that the story's "deepest meaning will be different for each person, and different for the same person at various moments in his life" (page 12).

We cannot go wrong by feeding our children the whole bread of Bible stories.

Presenting Stories

In most primary school classrooms, teachers set aside part of the day for reading stories to the children. And a large majority of these teachers will tell you that story time is the most popular segment of the day. Now, you won't want to read a sermon or a "lesson" to children, but you can read stories. It really is all right to do this, in spite of what you may have heard in the past. Many Sunday school teachers have always read stories. Some have had to close the door to do it, for fear a non-believer might see them.

When you read a story you should live it, just as though you were telling it. This helps you use expression naturally. Remember to read slowly enough that the children have time to hear every phrase. This is not an occasion to rattle off the words as you may have done at one time to impress your sixth grade teacher with your reading prowess. Remember the children before you. Look at them. Communicate the story to them.

Sometimes you may want to tell the story. Do this with a story that you love and know so well that it has become a part of you. Do it when you feel your telling will be better than the reading would be.

Visuals will help some stories; others don't need them at all. Children need some opportunities to make their own mental images. This is an important intellectual skill to develop. Children who have all their stories visualized on TV or on a flannelboard are deprived of good opportunities to grow in this way.

Flannelgraph visuals used during a story are helpful when the image must be built up throughout the whole story. An example is the story of Balaam who built altars on one mountain, then another, and then a third. These can be added as the story proceeds, and at the end are all three mountains with altars for the children to see. Each time the message was the same. God did not change His mind. And each time Balaam had to say, "God has not cursed the people; God has blessed the people."

A flannelgraph visual or a plain picture is used to good advantage when it gives children an image of something which is unfamiliar and which they are not likely to image correctly in their own heads. Fishing boats, priests, the temple and other such Bible items can come in this category.

Story sequence can be shown on a flannelboard. Instead of removing parts, changing scenes and so forth, with this technique you leave up a reminder of each part of the story. At Easter, for instance, you may show the cross, the closed tomb, and the empty tomb. After the story, the sequence is still there for the children to talk about and review. Primary children need much practice and experience with the concept of story sequence.

Stand-up visuals work best when movement is important to the story. An example is Joseph with Mary and baby Jesus traveling to Egypt and back again. Another example is showing what the high priest did on the Day of Atonement. He stands near the altar to kill the goat, he takes a dish of the blood into the tabernacle, and so forth. With a model tabernacle and a stand-up figure of a priest these procedures are shown clearly to children.

Puppets work best when there is a conversation. For instance, Abraham and "Lord" puppets can carry on this conversation.

"Will you destroy the righteous people with the wicked if there are at least fifty righteous in the city?"

"No, if I find fifty righteous people in Sodom I will not destroy the city."

"Lord, what if you can't find quite fifty righteous people? If there are forty-five righteous people will you destroy the city?"

And so on, down to the ten. Jesus and the woman talking at the well, or Jesus and Nicodemus talking at night are other conversations puppets can portray. Puppet visuals are not needed necessarily to help children make inner images of two people talking. Children can do this easily enough on their own. But the change that puppets bring to your story presentation will help children concentrate more on what is being said in the conversation. It's the variety that is effective here. Simple sack puppets or stick puppets that you make or that come with your lessons will do as well as expensive commercial ones. But if your church owns the expensive kind, by all means use them. Help your church get their money's worth out of them.

In summary, you can present stories by reading them, by telling them, or by using flannelgraph visuals or other visuals, or by using no visuals at all. There is no one best way to present a story. Children of primary age do not need to see everything in order to understand or remember it. The statistics you may have heard about the value of seeing are misleading. The real problem in story visuals is to select what best fits a particular story—what will best teach what you want to teach from it. Good curriculum materials will do this for you, providing you with a variety, and you can usually follow the suggestions in your lessons.

These matters of reading stories, telling stories, and using story visuals are treated at length in two full chapters of the kindergarten book in this series, and the reader who wants more information is referred to that source.

Preteaching

In classes where stories are enjoyed as stories there usually is no need for elaborate motivation gimmicks—such things as starting with some psychological need, to convince the child that it is worth his while to listen. A simple introduction may suffice: "Today we have another story about David," or "Do you know what a spy is? Our story today is about a spy."

Most children like to listen and intend to listen. What they need from you is help on how to do a better job of it. A simple and highly effective technique is to give them a listening task. They can listen to find the answer to a specific question. "Why did king Belshazzar lose his kingdom?" "Why did God send Jeremiah to the potter's house?" You might print the question on the chalkboard and ask one or more children what they are going to listen for. This gives everyone time to get the task set firmly in their minds. Sometimes the task may be in the form of a statement instead of a question. "Listen to find out something that

Ezekiel could do that you cannot do." "Tell what the important message was, and tell whether or not the people listened to it."

Sometimes the children can raise their own questions. In a unit about Elijah you might explain that now Elijah's work for God is all finished so "What do you think is going to happen to him?" Let the children make guesses but do not tell them whether they are right or wrong. Ask them to listen to the story to see if they are correct.

When you give a listening task before a story, don't forget to follow it up after the story. Give children opportunity to show that they found the answer. Discussion of the listening task comes first, and after that you can go on to other discussion you have planned.

Primary children can become quite proficient at listening tasks. One teacher puts on his chalkboard a long list of questions—maybe eight or ten. And after the story his children answer them. A fun variation is to tell the children that you will not ask any questions after the story, but they should listen and think of their own questions to ask the class.

Another variation is to appoint one or more official answerers. For instance, one child is to listen carefully so he will be able to answer questions about Mary, and another can listen carefully so she can answer questions about Martha. All the other children listen carefully too, because they must think up questions to try to stump the answerers. This is by far the hardest job. You should be ready with questions in case your children cannot do this well yet.

Children's understanding of many Bible stories is heightened with a little preteaching. Activities or visuals before a story are sometimes better than visuals during the story. An example is this preparation for the parable Jesus told of the wheat and the weeds. Demonstrate how a farmer sows his seed by hand. Or have a child demonstrate, if you have previously taught about sowing. Help the children observe carefully by talking about the demonstration. Did the farmer scatter his seed evenly on the ground or did it just fall in a bunch together? Did he take some steps so the second handful fell in a new place and not on top of the first? Did he take his handfuls from an apron that he held in front of him? Point out that the farmer learned to do all this smoothly and in a rhythm.

After noticing such details, let all the children get up and try to sow seed like the farmer. After a time you can delare that the field is all planted now and the children can sit down. If you don't live in a wheat-growing area you can also do some preteaching by showing pictures of wheat and weeds. Give a listening task. Say, "In this story an enemy sows. Listen to see what happens when the enemy sows."

As the story begins, the children will hear about the farmer sowing his wheat seed. Their minds will produce good mental images of what is happening—images that include the "feel" of the job and not only the "look." You can see now how this technique is superior to that of putting up a flannelgraph picture at this point in the story. If the children see the flannelgraph man with his hand outstretched and you teach at this time how people in Bible days sowed their seed, you will have interrupted the flow of the story and the children will have not as good an image as they would after trying out the sowing themselves.

As the story proceeds, the farmer goes to sleep. No problem with this image. There is no need to preteach it, and no need either to visualize it on the flannelboard. All the hired men slept too, and in the dark an enemy came and sowed weed seeds. A flannelgraph story can only direct you to take off one man sowing seed and to put on another man sowing seed. It's probably much better to leave the children with their own images of the enemy sneaking in the darkness. The story goes on with the wheat and the weeds growing up together. One day a hired man says, "Look." The men decide there's a problem and they discuss it with the farmer. Now how do you show a conversation on a flannelboard? The best you can do is to show men standing there, and perhaps a wheat field beside them. But what you really want the children to image is the content of the conversation. "Should we pull up the weeds?" the men ask. "No, let them grow together for now. At harvest time we can put them into piles and burn them. And the wheat can be stored in the barn."

Your preteaching on the unfamiliar images of sowing and of wheat will strengthen your children's understanding of this story. Children will internalize the story quite well, and be ready for this ending: When Jesus finished the story He said, "This story has a meaning. It shows how the children of God and the children of the devil will grow up together in this world. God doesn't take out the wicked ones now. But when harvest time comes, then all the wicked ones will be burned, and the others that God planted will be taken into Heaven."

"Do you understand?" Jesus asked the disciples.

"Yes," they answered. "We understand your story."

And your children will too.

Children with this lesson have help for acting mentally on the story. They make their own images. They have a listening task to heighten their concentration. It is a stronger lesson than if all the images are placed on a board before them and the children watch.

This preteaching could be called "readiness" if you prefer that word. But notice that it is a mental, or academic, readiness described here. It is not a psychological readiness of raising awareness in the children of a "need" or "felt need," so that the Bible lesson can proceed to reduce that need. Such psychological games are of doubtful value. Psychological growth, like physical growth, is not our major concern in the classroom. And even if it were, it has not been shown that this is the way to go about it. If you are concerned about the psychological needs of your children you will do fine with your commonsense human relationships and your Christian love for the children. And giving them success in their learning is important. This has been shown by research to be an effective psychological builder for children.

In summary, preteaching is effective when there are unfamiliar concepts in the story. This teaching can be in the form of visuals or activities, as in the preceding example. Or it can be simply verbal, such as learning a new word, talking about it, and relating it to familiar things.

Follow-Up

The next step after your story is to reinforce. Strengthen understanding by follow-up activities. Use different methods to go back over some of the important matters. Reteach. Repeat in new ways. A large proportion of the class time should be used for this type of work. Experienced teachers know this. Inexperienced teachers tend to think that once something is taught, it's taught and they can go on to the next thing. But give children more time and other ways to think about the lesson.

In a story about building the tabernacle, you may have used visuals as you went along, but don't stop with that. After the story, talk about the visuals. Let the children touch the parts and say the words—tabernacle, altar, curtain, most holy place. Ask questions and let the children ask questions. It's important that they talk about it, and not only you. Talk about "feeling" things too—the willing hearts to give, the joy at the work's completion. Can we have willing hearts too? Don't push these questions to the point of violating children's privacy, but allow opportunity for those who can and want to share feelings.

Let the children draw the tabernacle. You can show them how to make a floor-plan drawing, showing the holy place, and the most holy place, with the curtain between them. They can draw on paper or the classroom chalkboard or small individual chalkboards or Magic Slates. Let them describe their drawings. Pretend you are Mother or someone else who was not in the class and you don't know what a child's drawing is all about. Ask him questions and get him to explain it to you.

Practice a choral reading.

ALL: This is the thing that the Lord said to do,
      Bring some gifts and do some work too.
SOLO 1: I can bring gold.
SOLO 2: I can bring silver.
SOLO 3: I can saw wood.
SOLO 4: I can make metal.
SOLO 5: I can sew cloth.
ALL: We will do what the Lord said to do.

Play a game that will provide more drill on the special vocabulary of this lesson. (Several such games are given in Chapter 8 of this book.) Do some reading, as described in Chapter 3. Work on the sheets or books the publisher provides. Sing a joyful praise song. Have prayer time. Work on memory verses according to the principles described in Chapter 4.

All these follow-up activities strengthen the lesson. The Bible story is the center. Your preteaching starts off the learning, the Bible story does its work on many levels, the follow-up activities reinforce and build meaning. The multi-methods approach helps all kinds of children. Some learn better one way and some another.

Do you do all this in a class group, or with small-group or individual learning centers? Either way. If you have space enough and staff enough, and if you like managing this sort of thing, you can have a corner for drawing tabernacles, another corner for vocabulary drill games, and so forth. But if you prefer to lead the class together in their learning do it that way.

Some recent "super-research" compiled hundreds of available smaller studies comparing achievement in small-group and individual learning with achievement in whole-class, teacher-led instruction. The conclusion of the super-research was that teacher-led class instruction brings higher achievement. But the "small group" people argue that that's not true when the individualized learning system is used well. The problem, they say, is too many teachers are not using it well. So the controversy will not die and you can use whatever system you like and can manage well.

Do you have to plan all the activities and prepare materials for each of your lessons? You may have felt like asking this question much earlier in this chapter. The answer is No, you shouldn't have to. Sunday school teachers, club leaders, and others who do volunteer work with primaries usually have a family, a job, and other important life concerns. They should not be expected to give the huge amounts of time it would take to plan their own curriculum and lessons.

Even full-time professional teachers cannot do all of this planning work. An official of a large public school district reported that schools in his district do not each use their own curriculum. The school "administrators do very little inventing themselves," he said. "The development of a curriculum in any discipline is a rigorous process . . . ."

Good curriculum work takes staff and resources that your church likely does not have. So your denomination or your publishing house has done it for you. Your job is to take the lesson, see the value of its various parts, and fit the lesson to your particular children.

Your job is the most important in the whole line-up. You are the one with the actual contact and the teaching relationship with the children. Everything that went before—all the theological planning, curriculum planning, lesson planning, testing, art work, writing, printing—was looking forward to that hour you have with the children.

READING CHECK

1. One value of stories is that they make abstractions concrete. T F

2. Many stories clearly show good and evil as opposites. T F

3. Stories often contain "models" for children to emulate in their lives. T F

4. It is poor practice to read a story to primary children. T F

5. In primary classes every story should have visuals with it. T F

6. Preteaching some important concepts will help children get more from a story. T F

7. A listening task heightens the children's concentration on a story. T F

8. A compilation of many researches brings the conclusion that learning centers produce more learning than teacher-led, whole-group instruction. T F

7 Teaching with Art

- *Using Art Activities*
- *Abilities of Primary Children*
- *Encouraging Child Art*
- *Art Media*

Using Art Activities

Art has been assigned a wide variety of jobs to accompany Bible teaching—all the way from being a time filler for the last few minutes of the lesson period to a sort of magic "doing" or "applying" the lesson. It can perform quite well the job of time filler, but rarely does it enable children to "do" the lesson. If we had a Bible verse which said, "Thou shalt praise the Lord with color and with drawing," then a crayon or paint activity would be an ideal way to apply that Bible lesson.

Art sometimes is called "expression." That is, teachers want children to express what they have learned, through art media. It is true that children can show some things they have learned by drawing pictures. But most primary children are more advanced verbally, and can show you their learning by verbal means more easily. Some teachers use the word "expression" to mean that children can express their feelings through art. They can express their joy or sadness or hostilities. In some cases this is a useful role for art. A more common expression use in day to day art education is expressing the aesthetic self. This probably is the most legitimate expression use for art. Growing aesthetically is what art education is largely about.

Most Bible teachers probably do not want to be art teachers and do not want to play Amateur Psychologist. They simply want to use art in ways that will strengthen their lessons. This is a realistic and attainable goal. Art activities can help children think about the lesson. It gives another perspective added to the verbal, musical, visual, movement, and other kinds of lesson activities.

When children are drawing a chariot, they not only are showing what they have learned about chariots, but they are learning as they draw. How big should the chariot be? What shape? If the chariot is going to go it has to have wheels. How big should they be? Where should they be? How many? Or if it's Elijah's chariot going up, will it have wheels or not? If a horse is going to pull it how will the chariot hook on to the horse? Will it have a covering to keep out rain or hot sun, or will it be open?

If a child is going to set down his idea of a chariot, he needs to make lots of decisions. A picture must be in his mind before he starts, but after he starts he will run into details he hadn't thought of before. His idea of chariot is sharpened as he works on his picture. Drawing is learning.

The child, of course, does not necessarily work out his chariot problems correctly. But as he has opportunities to see chariot pictures, play Chariot, answer questions about a chariot, and draw more chariots, he will keep improving. That is your main teaching job in this case—to teach about chariots themselves and not the How-To of drawing chariots.

The child's drawing ability is in his head, not his hand—after certain minimum motor skills, of course. So your teaching should be aimed in that direction. The child who is actively thinking and solving problems while he draws will not be a discipline problem to you. The child who is not allowed ideas of his own, but has to copy your drawing, may be a discipline problem at times, especially if he has to do too much of this. (A fuller discussion of copying drawings, and research on the topic are presented in the kindergarten book of this series.)

In school art, children usually draw what they know well—themselves, their families, friends, pets, nature. Sometimes teachers take them on field trips—the zoo, the fire station, the airport. These first-hand experiences stimulate art. In Bible teaching classes we may feel somewhat limited in the first-hand experiences we have to use. We cannot take a field trip to a Galilee fishing boat, or visit the museum of angels. But some lessons can use family pictures and nature pictures. The child can draw himself obeying mother or helping a friend. He can draw some of the beautiful things God has made.

School art also makes use of the vicarious experience of stories. Children draw an episode of "Goldilocks and the Three Bears" or of "Ali Baba and the Forty Thieves." This use of art in Bible teaching has tremendous possibilities. Teachers who become skillful at this can make exciting lessons. Instead of showing ready-made visuals with all the stories, they stimulate the children to visualize the stories themselves.

One teacher, after the story of Elijah's translation said, "I wonder what the chariot and horses looked like. I don't think I'd know how to draw that."

"I do. I do," piped up Bobby excitedly.

"You do? How would you make it?"

"Like this (draws with his fingers). And fire coming out here. And it would go up."

"Would you have wheels on it?"

"Yeah. Big ones, like chariots have. There's fire on the wheels too."

"Well, Bobby," the teacher said, "you make us a chariot. Now, what else do we need if we're going to show this story?"

"Me too." "I'll make a chariot, too," said Kevin and Britt.

"Okay. Now what other pictures could we make?"

The children went on to plan pictures of Elijah and

Elisha walking, the river parting, the coat falling on Elisha. They took turns hitting the floor with a coat so they could see how it looked and felt when the prophets did it. When most of the children seemed ready to start, as Bobby was, the group went to the table and began their pictures. The children's enthusiasm and the teacher's gentle questioning soon got the slower children started too. Each child printed a sentence on his paper to tell what was happening, and a committee of two later arranged the pictures in order and hung them on the wall. The teacher chose capable children for that job because arranging that many pictures is a complex task for primary children.

The next week the teacher read the story to the children from their own pictures on the wall. During activity time various children could be seen looking at their own and at friends' pictures. Some read the whole story, walking along the wall as they did so.

That teacher remembers with a shudder the days when she provided outline pictures for the children to color. "Horrors," she says. "My children were thinking about the lines and staying inside them, and being neat, and they weren't thinking about the story at all." She laughs and adds, "I mean that's what the docile ones did. The others threw crayons and things like that."

Abilities of Primary Children

Art theorists, who study the development of children's art, are likely to be "purists" who would prefer to see art develop independently of other school learning. That is, they don't want it to be corrupted by its uses in subject matter teaching, poster contests, and holiday decorations. Making turkeys by drawing around the hand is anathema to these people.

And they don't want adult interference. They speak of "self-taught" art and the "aesthetic development" of children. They see this development as being hampered when children try to draw things realistic and recognizable and pleasing to adults.

Yet practically all teachers make use of art in subject matter teaching, just as they make use of reading, writing, singing, and other skills. This is called integrating the curriculum. The developing skills are used in purposes besides the "pure" one of developing the skills and abilities.

In your classroom at the present time you are highly unlikely to have a child who has not already had much adult "interference" with his developing art ability. So at least you don't have to worry about being the first to spoil the pristine art of a child raised and taught by purists. But if you use much art in your classroom, you will influence in one direction or another according to your own beliefs and the attitudes you show toward the child's work. So you will want to give some thought to primary art.

Children entering primary grades at age six have usually been through the scribble state of drawing. And they have developed a number of symbols—ways to picture man, tree, house, flower, and so forth. And most are into the pictorial stage—where symbols are combined into pictures.

The very young primary child may still be using a human symbol in which the head is most important, and thus very large. Some children make, instead, a large body with a "pinhead" at the top. Later on, arms and legs come into more importance, arms at first sticking straight out from the body. Still later, hands can do things and hold things. The first humans are practically all front view, but by third grade, many are in profile and are active, doing things.

Animals are introduced in kindergarten and first grade, and seldom appear in children's pure or self-taught art. So animals are shown in profile, as the adults have taught. Even though in straight profile, they often have all four legs.

When children begin combining their symbols into pictures, the items are typically arranged along a "ground line" or the edge of the paper, which serves as a ground line. A strip of sky and a sun are typically added at the top of a picture. By later primary years the sky may be colored a bright color all the way down to the ground line. Clouds, stars, rain, or snow may be shown. Each piece typically stands separately in the picture, although by later primary ages there is some overlapping to show items behind each other.

The various symbols the child has learned are treated almost as formulas, so that when they are combined in a picture there is little attempt to relate them proportionately. For instance, the formula house is made with its chimney and door and other parts. Then the formula people are added, and there is no thought given to whether the humans could fit in the doorway. Later there is some adjusting of sizes, so that a flower is not as big as a tree. Much of the adjusting seems to be for aesthetic effect, for arranging the space well. Children do know that houses are much bigger than humans, but few teachers urge that kind of realism onto the children. Most feel that the art would then lose much of its charm and aesthetic quality.

Children use ingenious devices to show what they want to show. A child may make a ground line and draw one side of the street, then turn his paper and make the other side of the street. He may turn his paper four ways to draw people sitting around a table. When they begin thinking about distance, children may place one item above another on the paper. Or they may draw a second ground line so the more distant, smaller items can be on it. They may show three sides of a house, looking as if two outer sides need to be folded back. And they would draw the fourth side, too, if they could figure out a way to do it. They may show both the inside and the outside of the house in the same drawing.

For a child who has not been inhibited along the way, anything that can be thought of can be pictured. Children will unhesitatingly draw many ideas that capable adult artists would balk at.

Franz Cizek, the Austrian teacher who first "discovered" child art, said, "Child art is an art which only the child can produce." When the day comes that children are copying nature too faithfully, and seeing things through adult eyes, the charming child art is forever lost.

Encouraging Child Art

"Don't make the grass red." "Our church doesn't look like that." Few teachers would make such blatant criticism of children's work, but many are genuinely puzzled about what they should say. They want to do something to encourage the child's best work. Praise of some things and not others implies a criticism of the work not praised. Even "Tell me about it" is not entirely safe because it can imply that the child's drawing is not obvious or understandable to you. Some teachers try, "Would you like to tell me about it?" This seems to save face because a child does not have to respond. One child answered, "This is not a story to tell, it is a picture to look at."

Of course if you're not doing "pure" art, but are illustrating a story of Elijah, the picture will have a story. You may ask, "What do you want me to write on your picture?" or "What are you going to write on your picture?" "Very interesting," "Nice colors," and "I like that" are brief, useful comments. Everything a child really tries at should be accepted. If he can't do better now, the only way he'll ever do better is to experience this acceptance and to continue trying in the future.

There is little point in stressing such things as neatness and accuracy. Children may respond by fearing your disapproval, and with fear they cannot do their best work. Besides, such features of children's work are largely determined by their coordination and level of understanding, and admonitions from you will not help this growth.

During the actual working period on art projects, it is distracting if you hover over the children and talk about their work. Your best place is more in the background, available and ready to help those who need help.

When a child gets an idea in his head and starts to draw, he needs time to finish his project. If he has to put it away and get back to it another time he will have forgotten by then his original idea.

Children who have trouble with an assignment may need more experience with the story or topic. You may be able to help with that experience. If that's not feasible, you might allow him to switch to another topic. Children who are insecure and can only draw the same things over and over need much help over a long period of time. You can allow them the security of familiar drawings, and at the same time gently encourage them to try new things. A happy classroom atmosphere and the enthusiasm of other children are helps in these situations.

And of course you don't really have to require art work of all the children. A project such as the Elijah story described earlier may require taking down some earlier pictures to make room for these. It may need a title. Children can contribute to the project by doing these jobs. If children read or listen to tapes they are learning too.

Art Media

With primary children you should not feel constrained to look always for new and clever little handcraft ideas. When children have a good challenge, such as drawing the chariot of fire, they will do better with a familiar medium. Something clever and new turns attention to the novelty itself. With each new medium, children need time to manipulate and explore its uses before they can do good representational work with it. Novelty has its uses, but it can be overdone.

Listed below are some of the common art media used in primary rooms.

Crayons. The most common, easily stored, easy-to-use drawing and coloring material. Have enough for all your children. This is not a good place to teach sharing. Waiting for turns and fighting for colors is destructive to the art work. It really is not more expensive to have enough crayons. Twice as many crayons last twice as long, so the cost evens out.

Broken, peeled crayons can do many things that whole, pointed ones cannot. Use the sides to color large areas quickly with delicate color. Sweep upward to make tree trunks. Twist to make furry little animals.

It is difficult for children to keep crayons unbroken for long. Grady was coloring hard and his crayon broke. He looked up with fright in his eyes and "confessed" to his teacher. "Oh that can't be helped," she said. "Crayons always break after we use them awhile." Then she helped him peel some paper off the longest piece and get going again. Children have enough worries and fears in their lives. Let's not add unnecessary ones.

Felt Pens. Because the color is more brilliant than crayons, children like to draw and color with these. Many classrooms provide them as routinely as crayons. But they are more expensive.

Paints. Only opaque paints, such as tempera, should be used. Water colors are for more advanced ages. Paint smocks are a must. A sink in the room is convenient, but teachers do figure out ways to get along without one. Brushes are collected in a can to be washed later. A partner accompanies each child as he goes to the lavatory to wash his hands. The partner opens doors and turns faucets so the painter touches nothing until he gets his hands clean. Wet paper towels take care of many wiping tasks, including hands which have only a little paint.

Using paints takes careful classroom management. You will want to think through all the procedures beforehand instead of waiting until you are in the middle of a mess.

A somewhat neater way to use paints is to put them into cleaned, roll-on deodorant bottles. The paint must be thinned enough to work well in the bottles, and this makes them a little less bright than brush work.

Chalk. White chalk for snow pictures, and colored chalk for other things. Primary children sometimes use chalk, but dust is a problem, and they are not entirely happy with the delicate colors. Wetting the paper or the chalk helps both problems. Try soaking chalk for a few minutes in a solution of one part sugar and three parts water. This will surprise you with chalk almost as bright as paint. Redip the chalk when it dries out.

Construction Paper. Children can cut out people, houses, trees, and so forth to arrange into pictures. This is an easy way to have children work together on a mural. For instance, you or one of the children can make Mount Sinai, and all the children can add people crowded at the foot of the mountain. If your children haven't done this kind of work before, you can demonstrate how you will fold paper in half, draw half a person and cut it out. Then let the children do their own and have all the variety in your mural that the children produce. Leaving the folds slightly bent adds a three-dimensional look to the mural, and you may want that occasionally. But plain, flat pictures and murals will be the mainstay of this kind of work.

Construction paper is also used for "paper sculpture." Any kind of stand-up or hanging item can fit this category. Roll a piece of paper for the body of an animal. Add head, tail, mane and other characteristics, and rolled legs. Make trees stand up by cutting a bottom slit in one tree, a top slit in another, and assembling the two. Curls, folds, cuts, and assembling of all styles can be used. It is a mental challenge to children to invent their own ways to make things they need for their Bible town or other project.

Boxes. With boxes and other construction materials children can make Bible houses and even whole towns. Some children love to work in three dimensions, and do quite well with this medium.

A single box can be set up to display a diorama. For a diorama, one side of the box is left open and a scene, usually three-dimensional, set up inside. Another kind of diorama leaves only a viewing hole on one end and a small light hole on the top. The hole for light can be covered with colored or white tissue paper to let in a subdued light. The scene to view is painted inside the box, sometimes with certain items standing in front of it for a three-dimensional look.

Boxes can also form a stage for puppets, or a theater or TV set for viewing stories placed on rolls of paper.

Clay. Practically all primary children love to model clay. Be sure the kind you get is soft and pliable enough for small hands which are not as strong as yours. Clay can be kept moist and reused many times, or items can be dried and painted, and even baked. Manufacturers include full instructions for uses of their clay.

Sometimes your project will need plaster of paris or other casting mixtures.

Here is a recipe for play dough you can make at home.

    1 1/2 cups flour (not self-rising)
    1 cup salt
    1 tablespoon powdered alum
    4 tablespoons vegetable oil
    1 cup boiling water
    food coloring or poster paints

Mix the dry ingredients. Add oil. Add boiling water, stirring vigorously until mixture holds together. Knead until smooth. Add color. This dough will last a long time when kept in an airtight container. Dried pieces can be painted with either tempera or enamel.

Paste and Glue. Some primaries can manage individual glue bottles, getting the holes open again each week. But if this battle with the bottles is too disruptive in your class, use a large bottle instead, and pour small amounts into jar lids or onto paper. Let the children use paste brushes with this.

The same advice can go for paste. If your children can manage the stiff commercial paste and plastic spreaders, you can use those. Otherwise, look for softer paste and use brushes with it. Here is a recipe for homemade paste.

> 1/3 cup flour (not self-rising)
> 2 tablespoons sugar
> 1 cup water
> few drops oil of peppermint or wintergreen

Mix flour and sugar. Add water gradually, stirring vigorously all the time. Cook over low heat until clear, still stirring. Remove from heat.

A brush or spreader works with this paste. It is good paper paste for small children.

Tape, Staples. Scotch tape and staplers are essential in classrooms where you do any amount of handwork. Children never need to be told how to use these. In fact, your real teaching job, in construction projects especially, will be to show them alternative ways to hold things together—such as interlocking slits. Primary children would hold the whole world together with tape if you let them.

With all art media—and other classroom supplies too—you need to use your best classroom management skills. Have enough materials for all, or else arrange for turns—as at a painting easel. You can have a smooth-running session in which the children concentrate on their work or you can have a session of bickering over who has the red, and where are the scissors. Don't try to solve the bickering by expecting the children to do too much waiting and sharing. Solve it, instead, by better planning on your part.

In your planning, allow for the children to do as many things as they can. If all the children must sit still while you pass out paper and scissors and crayons, this leaves them with unproductive time on their hands. These are times when trouble can start.

Children can help pass out things to speed up the process. Better yet, is some arrangement where each child can get and put away his own supplies. Perhaps each child can have a box with crayons, scissors, pencil and glue bottle. Or perhaps they can begin drawing and each child get up for scissors when he is ready to cut out his picture. This avoids a crowd at the scissors box all at one time, and it gives children opportunity to move, which they need.

You will need to take into account the space and shelving in your room, the number of children, the materials you use most often, and other factors unique to your class. With all these considerations in mind make your own plan for managing handwork sessions. If problems erupt in class, don't be too quick to blame the children. Analyze the situation and see if it could have been avoided by better management. Modify your plan as often as you see a need for change. You may never feel that you have the perfect system, but you will be getting closer.

READING CHECK

1. Drawing is the best way for primary children to show what they have learned.   T   F

2. Children can tell better by words than by pictures what they have learned.   T   F

3. Children may learn about an object before they draw it, and they learn as they draw it too.   T   F

4. In children's early pictures a ground line is often low on the paper and a skyline high on the paper.   T   F

5. Children draw people as big as houses because they haven't learned about size.   T   F

6. Most primary children would have a great deal of trouble drawing angels or something they have not seen.   T   F

7. Primary children cannot easily pick up a half-done project and finish it another time.   T   F

8. Usually the best classroom procedure is for you to pass out all the art supplies.   T   F

9. Art periods are not good times to teach sharing and waiting for turns.   T   F

Answers: 1—F, 2—T, 3—T, 4—T, 5—F, 6—F, 7—T, 8—F, 9—T

8   Teaching with Activities and Games

- *Why Use Activities?*
- *Story Activities*
- *Reviews, Quizzes, and Memory*
- *Vocabulary Games and Activities*
- *Reading Games and Activities*

Why Use Activities?

One of the greatest differences between experienced and inexperienced teachers is that the latter are largely unaware of the amount of drill needed. If drill sounds like too old-fashioned a word, change it to reinforcement or repetition. Change it to activity or involvement. Let the children learn something one way, then another, then still another.

If drill can be made interesting and fun, children's concentration is higher, and their motivation too. Thus you actually achieve more learning than in the dull kinds of activities that we ordinarily think of when we hear the word "drill."

When you put an appropriate amount of activity into your class session there are some side benefits for you too. One is that your discipline problems will decrease or even disappear. Another is that you can see more clearly what your children have learned and what they still need to learn.

By teaching with activities you are mixing the major

modalities of learning—auditory, visual, and kinesthetic. Children who do not learn well by one mode have another chance to learn the material by a different mode. In all of this, keep in mind that it is not the doing or seeing or hearing that counts in itself. What really counts is the thinking. The whole trick in teaching is to get the children to think. So activities need to be planned carefully to promote the thinking you are after. The activities suggested in this chapter are often linked with a certain lesson or teaching, and when you use these ideas you need to adapt them to whatever you are teaching at the time. Once you learn to use a few of these you can add ideas of your own, and even come to invent new activities to suit your own teaching purposes. That is not as difficult as it may sound. But, of course, it does take time, and you can be glad if the lessons you use already suggest appropriate activities.

Why don't all primary teachers use activity? Some teachers feel that it is play and not learning, and in some cases they may be right. But in cases where the activities are carefully designed to fit the lessons, these teachers may just need to try them a few times to be convinced of their value.

Some teachers say, "I would like to use games but my class is too large." These teachers might profit from a visit to a class such as Arnold Cheney conducted in Miami, Florida. Dr. Cheney is an education professor during the week and for a time was second grade teacher on Sunday. His class grew to about seventy, many of them bussed children not regularly accustomed to Sunday school life. There was no song leader or opening assembly to take up part of the hour. There were no assistants to take attendance or to help with discipline. Now, what would you do, by yourself, for a full hour, in a room crowded with seventy second graders? Cheney's answer was to invent games to help hold the children's attention.

Some of the games had their playing parts up on a large bulletin board. A player from the girls' team or from the team on "this" side of the room came forward to make a play. All teammates watched breathlessly, hoping she would make the right move. Opposing team members watched, too, hoping she would miss. All were playing vicariously, thinking about Cain and Abel, or about Jacob and Esau, or whatever the topic of the particular game. Now, all seventy children couldn't get a turn, but that's beside the point. Plenty of thinking went on in that classroom, and that's where the learning is.

If you're wondering why Cheney's wife didn't help him out with that large class, well, she was in another room with seventy third graders. A former public school teacher, she invented games too. The games that Arnold and Jeanne Cheney invented are published in a primary curriculum they helped to develop, and some of them are included in this chapter as samples of good learning activities.

So if you have seventy children, or fifty or twenty, you can use games. And if you have two children you can use games too. All it takes is a little ingenuity to adapt. Game rules are not written on tablets of stone and it is perfectly legal for you to change them to fit the size of your class.

Change the rules to fit the ability of your children, too. If they don't know well enough the words they are supposed to call out, write the words on the chalkboard and let the children look. If they can't read the cards they choose, let them choose anyway, and you read aloud for them.

Change rules to fit the space you have, too. If a game calls for a circle formation, but you can't manage that in your tiny room, will it work to have "It" come to the front of the class instead of the center of the circle? If the game or activity calls for movement from place to place, can it be done with each child staying in front of his own chair? Children can walk "in place" and get all the way from Jerusalem to Jericho if necessary.

Some teachers who claim they have no space, actually could find it if they looked around. Many Sunday schools have a large assembly room where the primary department meets for twenty minutes. Then classes disappear into their own little cubicles for forty minutes, and the large room is unused during that time except perhaps for a secretary or two counting up the attendance cards and the money. If one brave teacher upset tradition and took her class out there for an activity that needed lots of space, some other teachers might catch on too. Soon the secretaries could have another job—that of scheduling who gets to use the room and when. And that would be an advance.

Could a hallway or other space in your church be used for a time? In good weather an outdoor space will often serve your purposes.

Another objection sometimes heard is, "We just have curtains for walls, and I don't want to disturb the next class." In this situation , perhaps the worst thing you can do is to keep all your children perfectly quiet while you do all the talking. Then your voice will compete with the other teacher's voice and children will have difficulty concentrating on only one of the two voices. Research has shown that the children next door will have an easier time hearing their own teacher over a babble of voices than they will in sorting out her voice from just one other voice. Of course you don't want the babble to become too loud. Here again, rule changes can come to your rescue. Maybe the point can go to the first one who whispers the answer. Instead of clapping hands and stamping feet, how about wiggling a finger or touching the head?

There is still another reason why some teachers do not use the more active ideas in their lessons. One set of first grade lessons suggests that the Red Sea be chalked or taped onto the floor or parking lot pavement. Then from week to week various activities are suggested that reinforce the lessons about crossing the Red Sea and traveling through the wilderness. A department superintendent who was a professional teacher during the week said, "Here is all that good motor learning in the lessons, and my teachers aren't using it." Did they feel uncomfortable and silly with it?

Were they not convinced that it would produce real learning in their children? Did it seem beneath their dignity and childish to engage in such activities?

These objections often dissolve with just one good demonstration or participation experience. An enthusiastic teacher or the superintendent in such a situation can prepare one of these lessons and teach it to a group of children while the other teachers observe. Or the other teachers may become the "pupils" for the lesson. Once the teachers loosen up and actually go through some of these activities they feel more comfortable trying them in their classrooms.

Now, if such activities are new to the children, they may need a little time to adjust too. At first some may be too timid to participate. Or, more often, they will act silly because they don't know how to handle the unaccustomed activity they are allowed. If this should be the case in your class, don't decide too soon that it didn't work. Make new rules to tone down the silliness and try again another week. After a time you and the children will have worked out together the right way to use activities in your class.

The rest of this chapter gives ideas for games and activities. There is an attempt to classify them according to whether you wish to teach words (vocabulary), give practice on reading, reinforce the Bible story, or review. Any classification of activities can be only approximate; there is much overlapping of purposes here. But this arrangement will be a bit more useful than a completely jumbled one. Art activities are in another chapter.

This collection of activities is far from exhaustive. All that such a listing can do is to suggest some of the kinds of things you can do with your primary children to help them learn. Creative teachers can invent activities to go with their lessons. But thinking them up and preparing the materials is often more time-consuming than busy teachers can afford. Activities like these will be included in good primary curriculums to save you time. When you need to plan a lesson yourself, or supplement the curriculum you have, you can draw from these ideas.

Story Activities

Action Stories. Some stories lend themselves to pupil participation. For example, with the story of Peter's release from prison, explain to the children that they are to do what Peter did in this story. You will pause each time and wait for them. Then as you read or tell the story, pause for these actions: sleeping on the prison floor, getting up, dressing, following angel, knocking on door, knocking again, raising hand for quiet.

Sometimes instead of action, use speaking. The children can join on repetitious parts, such as Pharaoh saying, "No, I will not let you go."

Find the Mistake. After your lesson try this listening and thinking game. Make a statement about the lesson but put a mistake in it. The children are to find the mistake. Have teams and keep score if you wish.

After the children understand this process, some of them may be able to make statements with mistakes in them. Older children may even be able to take turns, each one who finds a mistake being the next one to make the statement.

Good Shepherd. With this story you can use a follow-the-leader game. The good shepherd calls one or more children by name. They follow him and do what he does. The bad shepherd calls, but no one follows. Let each shepherd take several turns.

Lost Sheep. With this story use a hide-and-seek game. Have a shepherd leave the room. While he is gone hide one child, who will be the lost sheep. When the shepherd returns he should look at all the "sheep" he has and name the lost one. Then he can look for him.

If your room has no hiding place, you may have the shepherd hide his eyes while you point to one child and he sneaks out of the room. The shepherd then opens his eyes and tries to name the lost sheep. He then goes out to find him.

Play the Story. There are a wide variety of ways to play the story. Sometimes the activity can resemble roleplay. For example, after the story of the Pharisee and the publican a volunteer can act out how the Pharisee may have prayed. He can do this without speaking, as a pantomime, or he may say in his own words some of the things the Pharisee prayed. Then another volunteer can do the same thing for the publican. Follow this with a discussion. Ask, "How did he make the Pharisee look proud? What did his hands do? His head?" and so forth. Then some other volunteers may wish to try it, and see how convincing they can make the character seem.

Sometimes the activity can resemble drama. Select various children for the various parts, and let them act out the story. With older children and with simpler stories the children may do this pretty much on their own. At other times you can give help as needed. Sometimes you can read the story, in full or in brief form, as the children go through the actions. They can try repeating this again without your reading, and adding speaking parts in their own words.

Still other times a play-the-story activity will have all the children playing the same part and doing the actions together. This will proceed much like a Pretend activity, with you leading and helping the thinking along. An example of this is described in the "Pretend" section which follows.

Pretend. Physical activity and some relaxation ideas can be gleaned from almost every story. Here is one example. After a story of the potter and the clay, ask the children to pretend they are clay and you are the potter. Say, "I want to make a thin vase," or "I want to make a ball." The children are to whirl around a couple of times and then try to make themselves look as much like the object as they can. Compliment one or more children on how round and ball-like they look. Spread the compliments around, making sure that you compliment each child at least once.

As a variation let a child be potter. He can name what

he wants to make, and then choose a child who looks most like that item. That child is the next potter.

Sometimes a pretend activity will follow the story more closely and be almost a playing of the story in which all pupils participate at once, playing the same part. For example, after the story of the four soils the children can all be seeds. Help them "think" the part by keeping up a running stream of talk yourself. Say, "Pretend you are a seed planted in the good ground. Can you make yourself into a tiny, round seed? Oh, I see some real tiny seeds. Now the sun is warm and you are feeling warm too. You are starting to push out one little sprout. Jerry's hand is his little sprout. I see some other arms starting to sprout too. Now you get a little bit larger. A leaf begins to open. You grow up slowly until you are as high as can be."

Try being seeds in the rocky soil or the thorns. Grow part way, then wilt and die. Finish this activity by being a seed in the good soil once again.

Pretend to be the farmer and sow seeds. Pretend to build the strong house on the rock, or be Noah and build the ark. Or pretend to be the ark floating around and finally bumping to a halt on the mountain. Be Abraham. Ride across the desert, wade through the river, climb over the mountains, and settle under the trees.

When these activities require moving about, you can call the game Space. Have each child get a space in the room where he is touching no one else. After an action where the children move (but do not bump into anyone), say "Space" and each is to return to his own space for the next story action.

Puppets. Use simple hand or stick or finger puppets to act out the Bible stories or parts of them. With more experience and with guidance from you, primary children can gradually improve their abilities with this. Simple stages or screens to hide the puppet operators enhance this activity.

For dialogues, spend time discussing with the children before they try the puppets. "What did Jesus ask?" "What did the woman say?" "What did Jesus say next?" When the children have the conversation well in mind, various pairs can try it out with puppets, using their own words.

Sometimes the conversations are in simplified form in the children's readers or study books. Children can read their dialogues from those. First study them well, and underline the speaking parts. When the children understand the conversation well enough two can use puppets and read the parts.

For more complex plays, help the children plan scenes. Ask "What happened first? What happened next?" List the scenes on a chalkboard. Decide together who is needed in each scene and talk about what they say to each other. Leave the list on the board so children can refer to it as their play proceeds.

Sometimes use puppets to say the parts in a choral reading or a chant.

Questions. If your general practice is to ask questions after the Bible story to check on listening and comprehension, try this switch. Before the story tell the children that you will not be asking questions as usual. But they are to listen to the story and think of their own quesions to ask the class after the story. After the story have the children's questions. Some children may enjoy coming to the front and being teacher as they ask their questions.

Thinking up questions is actually a more difficult task than answering them. So don't be discouraged if the children don't do too well by your standards. Commend them for the questions they thought up and give them more practice in other lessons so they can improve in this skill.

Ritual Games. Ritual games can be defined as a sort of stylized acting out of the story. To adapt this Esau-Jacob example to other stories you will just need to invent a new conversation which will enable the leaders to find those who belong to them.

This is how the Esau-Jacob game is played. Choose one Esau and one Jacob to come to the front of the room. Secretly tell all the other children who they are. You may whisper in their ears or pass out slips of paper. Give the name of Esau to one-half of the children and the name of Jacob to the other half. The original Esau and Jacob are each to try to find the other children who belong on his team. He finds out by asking two questions, so the conversation will proceed as follows.

ESAU (or JACOB):	What do you want?
CHILD:	I want the blessing.
ESAU:	Do you have hairy arms?
CHILD:	No, I do not have hairy arms.
	or
	Yes, I do have hairy arms.

After this conversation if the child belongs to the questioner he gets up and follows behind him, holding on to either the waist or shoulders. If he does not belong he remains seated. The questioner, with his follower, continues around the class trying to find all who belong to him. The game ends when no more children are seated.

In teaching games like this, do not expect the children to see the whole procedure ahead of time. Instead, go with Esau to a child and show them both what to say and do. When Esau can proceed on his own, do the same with Jacob. After learning the game, children will enjoy it even more a second and a third time. Choose new leaders each time. Simplify the game by having only one leader go to find his followers.

Roleplaying. Roleplaying is different from playing or dramatizing a story. In playing a story the children must follow the script, so to speak, and the result must match with the original story. In roleplaying, children are helped to take on various roles and the outcomes will depend on the participants. Here are some sample roleplay situations.

1) After the story of Belshazzar, his arrogance at the banquet, and his downfall, ask your children what they

think the next king would be like. Would he be more proud yet? If so, what are some things he might do? Or would he learn a lesson from what happened to Belshazzar? If he had a banquet would he thank God for the food and act differently than Belshazzar? Talk about these things until the children have ideas about how the next king would act at a banquet or other situation. Then let various children play the roles they perceive. Later you may want a lesson on how the next king did act.

2) After a lesson about Isaac and the wells, talk about some situations your children might experience in lines at drinking fountains, ticket windows, or check-out stands. What happens when someone tries to crowd in? Plan various situations with children trying to crowd in. Sometimes have "Isaac" lines which don't fight back. Sometimes have "I want my rights" lines which object to the intruder. After the roleplays talk about the feelings experienced and about pleasing God in these kinds of matters.

Share the Story. Use a picture of the day's Bible story or the child's take-home work, or other appropriate item. Pretend you are "Mother" and know nothing about the lesson. Ask a child, "Who is this? What did he do? What happened then?" and so forth, until he has explained his lesson to you. Repeat with two or three more children, as all the others watch. This is an ideal activity to do just before dismissal.

Show Me. This is a variation of Pretend or of an active quiz. Its inclusion here will demonstrate that there are no hard and fast rules about any of these activities. You can work out any suitable activity that helps to teach and that fits the level of your children, and you don't need to worry about whether it has an official name.

Here is an example of Show Me used after the story of the ten maidens and their lamps. Say, "Show me with your fingers how many maidens there were. Show me how many got in to the wedding feast. Show how your head nods and falls asleep when you wait too long. Show how you wake up when you hear a shout. How do you trim your lamp before you go out? Now show me how you follow the bridegroom. I will be the bridegroom." Lead the children for a walk around the room and then into the "wedding feast" (their own chairs).

Traveling. This provides vigorous physical activity. In many stories someone travels somewhere—to the temple, to Jericho, to Bethlehem. Try to relate this game to your Bible lesson.

Have the children form a line to "walk to the temple," and tap two sticks together in a walking rhythm. After a moment change to one of the other commands suggested below, and tap an appropriate rhythm for each. It will be easier if you use the "walk" command between each of the more active ones.

> Walk to the temple.....................
> Run to the temple ....
> Skip to the temple. .. ..
> Take big jumps to the temple . . . . .
> Now hop to your seats . . . .

Writing. Small writing assignments are exciting for primaries. Choose five important words from a story. Print these on the chalkboard. Ask the children to write something about the story using all five of the words.

First graders enjoy learning to write single words or short sentences. Sometimes they can copy your sentence and sometimes they can make up their own. Be sure to use the style of printing or writing that is taught in your children's schools.

Reviews, Quizzes, and Memory

Active Answers. This is fun for all quizzes where there are a limited number of choices, such as true-false, or Mary-Martha. Sometimes try three answers, such as true, false, or not in this story. Plan a different action for each answer choice. For instance, raise the right hand for a true answer and raise the left hand for a false answer. Some other possibilities are: clapping, touching head or toes, standing, sitting, running to this corner or to that corner. The actions can be as quiet or as active as you wish.

If possible, have all the children answer at once. If your group is too large for all to do the more active answers you may let several children at a time show the answers. The other children will be "observers" who raise their hands if an answer is correct.

Drawing Review. Prepare several questions which can be answered with a simple drawing. Ask the questions one at a time and let the children draw their answers. Some examples are:

> What did Mary put baby Jesus in? (Manger.)
> What did the shepherd take care of? (Sheep.)
> What did the shepherds see one night? (Angel.)
> What did the shepherds find in a manger? (Baby Jesus.)

The children may all draw at their seats on paper or Magic Slates or individual chalkboards, and then hold up their drawings for you to see. Or you may call on volunteers to come to a chalkboard in front of the group and draw the answer while the other children watch.

Find the Answers. Prepare a list of questions which have one-word (or short) answers. Print each answer on a separate card.

Before the quiz spend time reteaching the answer words. Pin them on a bulletin board in alphabetical order. Help the children pronounce and read each word.

Ask a question and have the children raise their hands when they find the answer on the board. Call a child. He points to the word. If he is correct he may take the word to his seat. If he is not correct, call another child who has his hand up. After all the questions, the children will enjoy counting how many words they won.

A variation is to print the answers on the chalkboard. After each question let a child find and erase the word that answers it.

Hop-It Answers. For this review activity, you will ask

questions and the children will spell out their answers by hopping on letters. As this kind of review is outstandingly popular with children, you may wish to make a reusable letter chart from heavy plastic about fifty-four inches square. With a felt pen, make thirty-six letters and squares as shown.

v	P	O	t	d	w
i	a	s	g	u	e
m	r	e	c	j	l
t	v	b	o	F	x
d	g	l	l	s	k
z	n	u	n	P	b

For one-time use you make chalk letters on the floor. (These need to be repaired occasionally during the review.) Or you may make letters on a sheet of butcher paper.

Ask a question. Let a volunteer show a one-word answer by hopping on each letter that spells the word. You say each letter as he hops on it. If he needs help, let another child show him where to go, but no one is to say the answer aloud. Continue in the same manner with the rest of the questions.

Memory Spots. Touch a spot in your room, such as the doorknob, and say the first phrase of your memory verse. Example: "Oh that men." The children all walk to touch the spot and say the phrase as you did. Or if your class is too large for this, let several children do it as the others watch. When all are seated again, tell them to watch carefully as you do two things. Do the first spot as before, then go to a second spot in the room and say, "would praise the Lord." The children do it after you. Continue until the whole verse is recited in this way. Caution the children, "It's getting longer now. Watch carefully."

This method encourages high concentration, since the children know they will have to do what you do. It allows time for mental rehearsal, an important feature, as explained in the chapter on memorization. And it uses the three major modes of learning—auditory, visual, and kinesthetic. So it will help each of your children learn in his best way.

For younger children three spots may be all they can handle at first. Older children may do about six. Sometimes you can make "spots" which are illustrations of the first word of each phrase. With these helps children will be able to learn longer verses.

Picture Review. Use a number of pictures about your recent lessons and prepare one or two sentences about each. Spread the pictures face up in a row on the floor. Seat two teams in rows on either side of the pictures, and about five feet back. Give each child a number. The first two children facing each other will be number 1 on their teams. The next two will be number 2, and so forth. If there is an extra child have him be scorekeeper.

When the teams are ready, read a sentence and quickly call a number. The two children with that number are to stand and try to find the correct picture. The one who picks it up first gets to keep it for his team. If you have a second set of sentences, the game may be played again with those. Then you may repeat the first set again.

Pictures can be mounted on cardboard for durability. Or the rule may be that players simply touch the picture and a referee names the winner, who gets to pick it up.

Remembering. Use a set of words or a set of pictured single items, such as shepherd, staff, sheep, oil, and so forth. "It" goes out of the room. The rest of the class decides on one item to remove. It returns and tries to guess which item is missing. If he misses, he can be It and try again. If he is correct, he can choose the next It.

Another way to do this is to have all the children close

their eyes while you remove a picture. Have them open their eyes and see if they know what is missing. Besides pictures, you can use sets of objects which help to teach a concept, such as carpenter's tools to help teach what a carpenter does, or household tools to help teach what a mother does.

Reverse Quiz. Let the children ask you questions. Make small cards with a name on each of a person or object from your lesson. Form two teams. Hold a card in your hand and let a team ask you questions that you can answer by *yes* or *no*. One team asks questions until they get a *no* answer. Then the other team asks. When a team guesses the name they win the card. Continue until all cards are won.

You can use a name more than once. For instance, with Samuel, Eli, and Hannah make three of each and have nine cards. Make a rule that no questions can be used more than once.

Stick Man Review. Have ready a list of questions. When the children answer one question draw the head of a stick man, when they answer a second question draw his body. Continue until all parts are drawn.

The man may be said to represent a Bible character the children are studying, such as Moses, or Peter. For older children try having two teams and ask questions of each team in turn. See which team completes their stick man first.

A variation is to have a teacher drawing and a class drawing. Each correct answer earns a line on the class drawing, and each missed question earns a line on the teacher drawing. See whose drawing is completed first.

Sometimes draw a church or other item instead of a stick man.

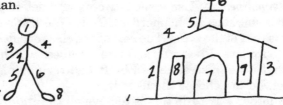

Tic-Tac-Toe. Prepare a list of review questions. Draw a Tic-Tac-Toe grid on the chalkboard. Form two teams—an X team and an O team.

Ask the questions in turn. Call on a volunteer from the team whose turn it is. If he answers correctly he gets to mark an X or O in the square he wishes. The team that first completes a row vertically, horizontally, or diagonally is the winner.

Two Tries. This may not qualify as a game or an activity, but it is an extremely effective paper and pencil way to learn from quizzes. Read approximately five questions and let the children write their answers. Then read the five answers while each child checks his own work. The children turn their papers to the other side, you read the same five questions again, and the children answer again. The second time almost everyone will have their answers right. Those who miss will probably only miss one. See how easy it is to learn?

Vocabulary Games and Activities

Basket Upset. Use about three or four words you wish to teach. Make several cards or small slips of paper for each word, and prepare sentences ending with each word.

Arrange the children's seats in a circle. Pass out one word card to each child. Make sure each child knows his word. Whisper the word to those who need help reading them. Remove one chair and have that child stand in the middle as "It." Read a sentence, saying the last word louder. On that signal all who have the word try to exchange seats with each other before It gets a seat. A child left without a seat becomes It for the next turn. After a few turns, have the children exchange words for further play. Sometimes instead of reading a sentence, call all the words for a "basket upset."

Categories. This game is good when you want to contrast or differentiate between any two characters or ideas. Examples: Cain and Abel, Elijah and Ahab, Saul and David.

Make two headings and make an equal number of cards to go under each heading. Examples: Abel—shepherd, obeyed God, offered a lamb, God was pleased, not angry. Cain—farmer, did not obey God, offered food, God was not pleased, angry.

Pin the headings on a bulletin board. Scatter the cards face down on a table or floor. A child from the Cain team chooses a card. If it belongs under Cain, he pins it in a column under the Cain heading. If it does not belong under Cain, he turns it face down again with the other cards. A child from the Abel team takes his turn in the same manner. The first team to get its cards in place is the winner.

Hopscotch. Spread words widely apart. Call two words. Volunteers must hop on one foot to the first word, straddle it, then hop to the second word and straddle it. Work up to three or four words to keep your children challenged.

Concentration. For this game you need pairs of word cards. Use words from the day's lesson or the current unit of lessons and print each word on two cards. When the words are objects, they can be illustrated with pictures—for instance: tabernacle, brass serpent, manna, Moses. An X card can be added for extra suspense in the game.

Mix the cards and turn them face down on the floor, table, a flannelgraph board, or a card holder. The first player turns up two cards. If they match he keeps them and takes another turn. If they do not match he turns them down again and his play ends. The winner is the one who has the most cards after all cards have been claimed.

Groups of up to about five can play this game as individuals. Groups of any size can play it in teams.

Sometimes you can add a rule that a child must read the word aloud or tell something about it before he can claim the pair.

Motion Spelling. A leader assigns an action to each of two letters in the alphabet. For example he may say, "For *e* you raise both hands and for *j* you stamp your foot." Everyone practices the actions briefly. Then the leader or teacher calls out a spelling word to the first player. The player spells it aloud, except for the motion letters that may be in it. For these letters he does the assigned action. If the player misses, he sits down. If he succeeds he becomes the new leader and gets to assign an action to a third letter. Players practice all three actions. A new spelling word is given to the next player. If your children are good at this you may let each new leader add another action, up to a limit of six actions. But three actions will probably be enough for many primary classes.

Word lists should be related to your lessons. The players can help you make a list by calling out words from the lesson, as you write them down. If you have a chalkboard the words can be written there for all to see. On a new, hard list players can do the motion spelling while looking at the words. When the list is more familiar, the player whose turn it is can stand with his back to the chalkboard while a word is called for him. Make the game easier by limiting the length of the words to five or six letters. Make it harder by using longer words.

Pass the Word. Have the children form a circle and pass out a word card to each child. At the signal "Go" they begin to pass their words to the right, and at the signal "Stop" they quit passing and hold the words they have at that time. You call one word and the child who has that word is to tell something about the word from the Bible story. Then he keeps it under his chair. Repeat until all the words are under the chairs. The children may enjoy counting to see how many words they have.

For classes smaller than your word list, give each child a word, then add a new word each time one is taken out. For classes larger than your list, some children simply start with no word.

Ring Match. Make pairs of word cards and draw a ring around one word in each pair. Six pairs of cards make a good size game. Illustrate the words when possible. An X card can be added for extra fun and suspense.

Mix the cards and turn them face down. Form two teams. A child from Team A draws a card. If it has a ring he tells something about the word and pins it up on his team's portion of the bulletin board. If it does not have a ring he turns it face down again. A child from Team B then takes a turn. As soon as a team has three ringed words (or half the total you have prepared) they begin trying to pair with them any matching words they draw. The first team to complete its pairs is the winner.

For a shorter version of this game, pass out the ringed cards at the beginning. Then let the teams draw to complete their pairs.

Scrambled Words. Make letter cards—one letter per card—for the words you wish to use. Use these in a pocket card holder or on a flannelboard. Show a scrambled word. Let the children try to find it in their books, and then unscramble it.

Let the children each take a letter of the word and try to arrange themselves in order.

Sentence Game. Cut out several pictures of people or items from your Bible lesson. Example: Moses, rod, burning bush, sheep, shoes. Mount the pictures on identical pieces of paper. Turn the pictures face down and scramble them. Let a child select two pictures and try to make a sentence using both words. After his turn he puts his pictures back and mixes all the pictures before the next child takes a turn.

Word Find. Use some Bible words you are teaching about in your current unit, and make a card for each. Circle cards would be an interesting change. Place the cards on a bulletin board or flannelboard, or on the floor.

Call a word and let a volunteer find it and pick it up. For first graders have a duplicate set and show them the word to pick up. Repeat until the words are learned well.

To make the game more difficult, call two words or three words and the player must find them in order.

After the children know the words quite well you can play an active game. Set the words on the floor and arrange teams on either side, or line the teams relay style and put the words across the room. Call or show a word quickly and the first child on each team races to pick up the word. Call again and the second team members run, and so forth, until all the words are gone.

Writing. Air writing is fun for primaries. Print your study word on the chalkboard. Then face the same direction as the pupils and all together trace the word in the air. Go slowly and say each letter as you form it.

A variation is writing on palms with index fingers. Print *sin* on one palm. Print *blood* on the other palm. Cover sin with the blood. Print a special word on the palm, close the hand and take the word home.

Another variation is to print a word on a child's back. Trace large letters with your finger, one at a time on top of each other. See if the child can name the word.

Reading Activities

Choral Reading. Use Scripture, or sometimes use a selection from the child's reader or study book. These will be in simpler vocabulary. Plan a choral reading arrangement of the selection. You do not need special training for this; simply decide on various parts that you think might sound nice. You can have a soloist read certain lines, and the total group read other lines. Further variations are to have a loud-voice group and a soft-voice group for certain parts. Or try high and low voices if you can divide your children that way. Or simply have two groups, perhaps on opposite sides of the room.

Practice reading the arrangement. Intensive practice on the parts, such as learning to emphasize certain words, pausing at certain places, and so forth, will help the children speak together. This also will make an enjoyable result for all participants.

Some selections may be read; others may be memorized. After some experience with this, let the children help plan the choral arrangements. Sometimes find an audience for these productions—perhaps another class.

Scrambled Story. Prepare several sentences which will tell your Bible story in brief form. Print each on a strip of paper and back them for use on a large flannelboard.

Scramble the sentences on the board, leaving as much space on top as possible. One child picks up the sentence he thinks belongs first and places it at the top. You or that child choose someone to come next and place the second sentence. Continue until the story is in correct order.

When a mistake becomes apparent, let the children reread the sentences and discuss and try different arrangements until they have figured out the proper order. Much learning happens in such situations. Even when there are no mistakes, each child silently reads and rereads sentences and thinks about their order so as to be ready for a turn.

Sentence Permutations. Have fun and lots of reading practice with some of the sentences in your children's books. Make a card for each word of the sentence and use them on a flannelboard or card holder. First have a child arrange the words as they are in the book. Then see how many other sensible arrangements the class can make.

> Example:
> Dorcas was alive again.
> Again Dorcas was alive.
> Alive again was Dorcas.
> Was Dorcas alive again?
> Dorcas again was alive.

READING CHECK

1. As teachers gain more experience they generally make less use of drill.   T   F

2. Activities often are simply fun drills.   T   F

3. Activities waste time that could be spent learning. T   F

4. One problem with activities is that they do not make enough use of listening.   T   F

5. Many activities provide a good mix of seeing, listening, and saying or moving.   T   F

6. Games cannot usually be used in large classes.   T   F

7. It is generally more difficult for children to make up questions than to answer questions.   T   F

8. Acting out a Bible story is roleplaying.   T   F

9. Competition heightens the interest in many games. T   F

10. Some primary activities can be successful with no competition at all.   T   F

Answers: 1—F, 2—T, 3—F, 4—F, 5—T, 6—F, 7—T, 8—F, 9—T, 10—T.

9 The Teacher

- *Physical Health*
- *Mental Attitude*
- *Relating to Children*
- *Self-Image*

Mrs. J. was fearful when she first took the job of teaching. She was afraid of the children and afraid she didn't know the Bible well enough to teach them anything. She studied the lesson materials faithfully and tried to do what she was supposed to. At first she thought so much about herself and how she was performing, that she couldn't have told you much about any of her pupils. But gradually they became real persons to her and she found she enjoyed being with them. Classroom conversation became genuine human intercourse. Mrs. J. feels she has learned a lot about the Bible in her two years of teaching, but she often worries about whether she is doing a good job. She thinks other teachers know what they're doing, and she is just an amateur never quite doing it right.

Mrs. W. has been teaching for thirty years. She always knows exactly what she will do in class because she has been doing it the same way for twenty-eight of those thirty years. At home she has a closet full of flannelgraph visuals, and if the lessons the superintendent gives her don't have flannelgraph visuals, she pulls some out of her closet and uses them. At times in teachers' meetings she has shown belligerence when they talk about other teaching methods. The superintendent sometimes refers to her privately as "the flannelgraph teacher." With her domineering manner she has good control in her classroom. She never misses a Sunday, and likes to think that more than three hundred children have gone through her classes over the years.

Mr. B. is a gregarious, popular person around the church. They talked him into teaching primary children by explaining that young children need male role models. He puts his lesson manual in his briefcase, along with his sales material, and sometimes on a plane flight he reads it awhile. But he thinks it doesn't matter much whether he studies; he can always "play it by ear." He doesn't prepare the visuals or other materials, but tells his wife she can if she wants. In class he sits at a table with the children and talks to them about the Bible story. The children are attracted to Mr. B. They listen and respond and ask questions. But after about twenty minutes the atmosphere grows quarrelsome. A child complains that his neighbor poked him. Another drums loudly on the table. Mr. B's cheerfulness comes to contrast more and more with the mood of the children, and soon he turns the class over to Mrs. B. for the activities she has prepared. Mr. B. thinks teaching is easy.

Miss F. is a high school student, overweight, and timid in her relationships with her own age group. She makes good grades and works hard on the school paper, decoration committees, and other activities that she takes on. She works very hard on her primary teaching job. She is always there early, mentally going through each activity and getting the materials for each arranged as conveniently as possible. She relates quite naturally to the children, talking with them just as she does with her younger sister and her friends. Once in a while when the children get too rowdy, she tries her "teacher voice" and tells them to sit down and be quiet. It works. And with her well-planned lesson she can get them going again on something they're supposed to do. Miss F. finds teaching very satisfying.

None of these teachers are like you, of course. If you

were to write a profile of you as a teacher, what would it say? Do you think you would be entirely happy with the results? Or would you rather make a few changes and then try the profile a few months from now?

You can't separate yourself as a teacher from yourself as a person. You are all of one piece. And it is good for your pupils that you are. They learn better from a human than from a teaching machine. But in thinking of your teaching profile you might try looking at a few pieces anyway. We consider here the pieces of physical and mental health, relationship with children, and self-image as a teacher. Spiritual maturity goes without saying, and you will want to include it in your profile of yourself, but we will not take on the task of discussing that here. Numerous other books, and the Bible itself, can be consulted for this topic.

Physical Health

Maybe you never thought of health as related to teaching, but for teachers of young, exuberant children robust health is a must. This means the rest, exercise, and good nutrition that you've always known you need.

Reed came early to Sunday school. He went down to the almost empty basement and saw his teacher there busily getting things ready. Playfully he hid behind a curtain for a while, peeking out this side, then that side. The teacher didn't enter his game so finally he jumped out and said, "Boo! Did you know I was hiding behind the curtain?"

"Yes, I saw you," she said with irritation. "What are you doing here so early?"

An observer could almost see Reed shrivel up inside. His teacher wasn't happy to see him. She didn't like his game.

Why did the teacher react that way? Was she up late the night before? Did she skip breakfast in the flurry of getting her own family ready? Maybe she needed more iron in her blood. Or if the reason wasn't physical, perhaps it had to do with personal problems and her emotional health.

Whatever the case, this teacher reacted in terms of her own needs. She was not on top of things enough to see Reed's need and to respond to that.

Improving the nutrition, getting to bed early enough on Saturday night (and every night), and all other good health measures are a service to God that teachers perform.

Mental Attitude

Insecurity, poor self-image, hostility and other mental health problems will also be hindrances to good functioning as teachers. Some attitudes may need to be faced as sin, confessed, and cleansed in the way God has provided. Others are overcome or improved by a slow growing process.

A special hazard of teaching is the strong desire for things to be better. Teachers dream for their pupils. All of them will be saved, they will learn to act like model children, and so forth. Then when the children fall short of the dream the teacher feels frustration and failure. Just knowing this characteristic of teaching is a help. Your vision and goals will always be out ahead, and the children grow slowly. Accept this as God's way.

Your own growth may seem slow too. Mrs. J., mentioned earlier, started out as a fearful, insecure teacher. She didn't give thought to her growth, but she worked hard and faithfully at her job and growth happened along the way. She can look back now and see that she has become a better teacher. If she could observe in other classrooms she would be even more encouraged. She would see that, though problems differ from class to class, there are always problems. She would see that, in fact, teaching seems to be made up of problems and the challenge of solving them.

A Sunday school teaching job often has the effect of isolating a teacher from the fellowship that could encourage her the most. This is particularly true in a small church. All the other adults are having a great discussion in their class (at least she thinks they are), and she is downstairs "babysitting" so they can do it. And since she is the only primary teacher, there are no primary department planning meetings, so she is left alone in the job.

In these situations, neighboring teachers can help each other in little ways that have big effects—for instance, the way they greet each other and go about their before-class chores on a Sunday morning. A teacher's attitude can say he's glad to be there, and it's all a worthwhile work. This, of course, should be genuine. An artificial Pollyanna outlook doesn't help the teacher who is feeling discouraged. If a teacher is lamenting that her chalk is gone again, you can't say, "Well, praise the Lord, all we have are little problems." This will make her feel put down for complaining. It's better to agree that the chalk is a problem and help her find some. This gives a real lift. If your job seems unexciting or discouraging at times, remember it may be for others too. You can help. And they can help you.

Relating to Children

The advice to "love your children" may not be over-worked advice, but at least it is ambiguous, and many teachers aren't sure what it requires. Some try to work up a feeling of love over charming characteristics of children, but this method leaves some of the children seeming unloveable. Some feel it means they should be constantly doing things with and for the children.

One public school first grade teacher found she "loved" her children so much that she wanted to take one or two home with her each weekend. Hers was a life where her only fulfillment came from teaching and from having the children like her. It was an unhealthy attachment. And a teacher counselor had to tell her firmly that she should find adult companionship for her weekends.

Teachers in Christian ministries can do many out-of-class things for their children, not as unhealthy need-fulfillment of their own, but as a way of showing Christian love to the children. Even so, many times there will still be a child or two that a teacher really doesn't like. What should the teacher do in such cases?

Some years ago it was fashionable to speak of "personality clashes." Teachers felt better with this psychological label. The name served to take guilt off the teacher if she didn't "love" a child. It wasn't her fault, after all. It was just one of those personality clashes. Teachers were even counseled to expect some of these and not to be too upset over them.

But one public school teacher of twenty-five years testifies that she never saw the personality clash that couldn't be overcome. She tells about the first child she found herself disliking. In a third grade class many years ago she had a boy named Gerald. She had always hated the name Gerald, so when it was attached to a boy who had a foul smell because of constantly running ears, she didn't like it any better. And her first general impression of him was of stupidity. She admitted being repulsed by the boy and she prayed that God would give her love.

Love didn't come the next day, but she carried out her duties anyway. She learned that the boy had only recently begun using a hearing aid, but always had had poor hearing. That accounted for his retarded speech and vocabulary development. The teacher planned special strategies to help him catch up. She learned how to help with his hearing aid when it acted up. As she worked and saw his progress she noticed one day that she was genuinely fond of him.

So that was how God answered her prayer. She tried to remember it through the years. Disruptive children, slow learners, unattractive children—all were challenges for her to show God's love by being the best teacher she knew how to be. Not every challenge had a storybook happy ending. Some she calls failures. But the very fact that she saw them as failures shows that she cared and she tried.

That is the way a teacher loves.

To examine your attitudes toward your own children, you may wish to try this exercise.

Step 1. Write out from memory a list of the children in

your class. If you are not going to do this immediately do not read Steps 2 to 4 but skip over to the next section, "Self-image," and come back to this when you wish to try the exercise.

Step 2. Do not read this step until after you have completed Step 1. The next thing to do, ideally, is to obtain a roll of your class and add onto the bottom of your list any names you did not include. If a roll is not immediately available you may proceed with the names you have.

Step 3. If your class is very small, take the top name and the bottom name for this step. If it is larger, take two or three names from each end of the list. There should be a large middle section left—at least half the class. Start with one of the names selected. Pretend this child is going to be moved to another class and you are going to tell the teacher about him. Write out your description so you can refer to it later. Repeat this process for each of the names selected. Do not read Step 4 until you have completed these descriptions.

Step 4. Analyze your descriptions. Are those from the top of the list longer than those from the bottom? Do they show more emotional involvement, indicating that you "enjoy" one child, or "put up" with another? If so, your responses are typical of many professional teachers. The first-named children are usually those the teacher interacts with most and knows most about. The last-named or forgotten children are closer to the edges of the teacher's awareness. This experience itself will have brought you insight and perhaps have already given you some ideas about what you should do.

Self-Image
Probably the greatest hazard to a Christian teacher's self-image today is the deluge of books, articles, and seminars which bombard the teacher from all sides with the "scientific" view of learning. The sheer bulk of it, along with

the general faith of our age in science as truth, is having its effect. Many teachers believe that "science" now "knows" how children learn and how we should teach. But the teacher never quite knows how to run her classroom scientifically. Or if she thinks she knows, it never quite works out as it seems that science should. And she often feels guilt or frustration over this.

Paul D. Ackerman, psychology professor and president of the Creation Social Science and Humanities Society, states that all scientific "personality theories are ridiculously inadequate" *(The Proceedings of the Sixth National Creation Science Conference*, Bible Science Association, 1979). He would not on this account dispense with them. These theories do "provide insights into narrow and limited domains of human behavior."

We can paraphrase Dr. Ackerman here, and speak of learning theories in exactly the same way. Scientific learning theories provide insights into narrow and limited domains of human learning, but when applied across general classroom teaching situations they are ridiculously inadequate.

Ackerman comments that psychologists, regardless of what personality theory they hold, conduct their own lives by a commonsense view of psychology. Good teachers do the same with their teaching.

Commonsense psychology has been held in low esteem while we all have been urged to adopt the scientific view instead. We can see this phenomenon more clearly if we use an example outside the fields of learning and psychology. Ackerman cites the example of the fossil record. The record shows that there are distinct kinds in creation, and this is what common sense would lead one to believe. But Darwin rejected the commonsense view, and interpreted the record as being evidence for an unbroken continuum leading from kind to kind in the evolutionary system. For decades people have been taught to distrust their common sense and to believe science instead.

Ackerman says his own view "is that the most correct and most valuable description of man's personality, apart from Scripture, is that provided by commonsense psychology. It is more useful and accurate in predicting and controlling behavior in general contexts than any of the scientific theories of personality."

The same could be said for teaching and learning. It is sobering to think that Augustine had a teacher, and Calvin and Luther. These teachers did not have the advantage of our twentieth century research on learning, but somehow their students managed to learn. It is not as though God has left us floundering for several thousand years, and now, in this century, we at last can learn how to use our brains.

So use your common sense without guilt. You are a human, made in the image of God, and so are your children. You know children in ways that only humans can. And you know what you hope to teach them. Science cannot work with "wholes" like this. It works only with bits and pieces of the learning process. You can add to your common sense some of those bits and pieces when—and if—they fit in. But don't abandon your common sense the way evolutionists do when they look at the fossil record.

Some in the scientific world are questioning, too, just how far all this scientism has brought us. Berliner and Gage, after reviewing the history of research on teaching methods conclude that "We should expect any teaching method to be about as 'good' as any other when the criterion is student achievement or knowledge or understanding, and the content coverage of the methods is similar. The data support this conclusion" *(The Psychology of Teaching Methods*, The Seventy-fifth Yearbook of the National Society for the Study of Education, 1976, p. 15). These writers go on to caution that this does not mean that different methods are equivalent in other ways. They may differ in time efficiency, cost, and motivation. They may differ in results with individual students. But when class averages are looked at, one method cannot be shown to be superior to another.

A dean of the University of Chicago Graduate School of Education, Philip Jackson, has a somewhat similar view of the research. He explored this topic a few years ago in a teacher's magazine article *(Instructor*, January 1975). "Are we making any progress?" he asked. Or are the changes "simply shifts of fashion"? He thought about good teachers of fifty years ago and realized that he would hire them if they came around today. In his more cynical moments, he said, he "would contend that fifty years of [research] has shown us one thing: that for teachers it is better to be nice than to be nasty!"

Jackson goes on to point out two major shifts in education, which he can classify as real development and not merely shifts of fashion. One is the waning of harsh treatment of children: rapped knuckles are out. The other is the decrease in rote learning: we no longer memorize state flowers. Even these two ideas, he recognizes, have been around since the very earliest education writings. But we now have clarified these fundamental ideas and accept them widely.

While secular educators wrestle with what the research means and where it has brought us, some Christian education writing, unfortunately, leaves us with another view of the research. One research study may be quoted, and that without enough details so that we readers might judge for ourselves what we ought to make of it. And from the quotation is derived something almost equivalent to a theory of teaching or learning. Of course a few Bible verses are thrown in for good measure. Bible verses are like research studies: you can take your pick and serve your purpose. Earlier we noted the "Visual Aid Theory" that grew up in this way. Other overly simplified theories of learning are now following this one.

Now, the point for any teachers who may have been somewhat intimidated by the scientific talk they hear is to have confidence in their own good common sense. Sunday school teachers have been doing lots of things right for several generations now. If we include Bible club teachers, camp workers, and others involved in Christian education of children in our society, this group has a part in the overwhelming majority of salvation decisions among our Christian population. Most church members owe a large part of their Bible knowledge to this teaching. They may not be able to name the apostles, as an occasional survey asks them to do, but they know how the world began, how sin entered it, how God judged with a flood. They know that God chose the Jews and sent His Son through them to be the Savior of the world. They know quite a lot about Jesus' life on this earth. They know especially about His death, burial and resurrection, and about His coming again. They know of Satan, Heaven and Hell, and eternity.

The students not only know most of these things, but practically all believe them to be true. And a good many order their lives differently because of them. Compare this result with the average person's learning from something else that he studied once a week—say health, or art or music.

Teacher, you have been doing a great job. You are one of the most important people in our society. You deserve a polished, red apple, and more.

READING CHECK

1. Problems are a sure sign of poor teaching.   T   F

2. Showing love and feeling love for the children may not always occur together.   T   F

3. People quite often are right when they use what is called "common sense" psychology.   T   F

4. In this century, research has shown us quite clearly what the best teaching methods are.   T   F

5. I feel better about my own teaching after reading this chapter.   T   F

Answers: 1—F, 2—T, 3—T, 4—F, 5—Hopefully your answer is T.

Appendix

In this appendix are the following kinds of study helps for each chapter. These may be used when this book is studied in classrooms or in church training groups.

Discussions: These items can be used as starter questions for class groups discussing this book together. They may also at times be used for essay topics.

Projects: These suggest further study beyond the bounds of this book.

Observations: These tasks are guides to help students focus on specific and meaningful occurrences, and thus to gain more from their observations.

CHAPTER 1: MEET THE PRIMARY CHILD

Discussion

1. Can you remember any times when an adult took action in a quarrel or other social problem you had as a child? What happened? What effect did it have on you? What can you learn from this experience for your own teaching?

2. Can you give Scriptural justification for either the teaching approach or the authoritarian approach to discipline—or both? What? Try to get beyond the usual few verses that are quoted regarding discipline. Broaden the discussion with other Scriptures and general Scriptural principles which you feel can apply.

3. Evaluate the developmental tasks against your personal growth experience. If you see any problems with the list discuss these with your class or study group. (If the group agrees a change or addition should be made you are invited to write to the author about it.)

Project

Choose one or two Bible stories and plan from each a moral behavior topic for discussing with primary children. The examples of Isaac and Abraham in this chapter are samples of the kinds of topics that can be used. For each topic give examples of reasoning at either Stage 1 or 2 and at Stage 3. Many primary children profit from exposure to Stage 3 reasoning, so this kind of preplanning can help you lead a good primary group discussion.

To carry the project one step further, give an example of Stage 5 or 6 reasoning for each of your topics. Primaries will not understand this reasoning, and being aware of it will help you learn to keep discussions with children on their own level.

Observation

Observe primary children at a playground. If they are involved in free play, notice what the boys choose and what the girls choose to do. What activities do they do in groups? Are there loners? What do they do? What quarrels or other problems do you see?

If the children are involved in planned group games, notice how well they cooperate. What problems in cooperation do you see? Notice incidents concerning good cooperation and poor cooperation. Do you see incidents of thoughtlessness toward others? Do you see incidents of consideration toward others? What action, if any, does the supervisor take to encourage this?

Share your observations with others in your study group.

CHAPTER 2: THINKING AND LEARNING

Discussion

1. What do you find helpful or satisfying about the developmental theory of learning? How do you think it might be useful to you in your teaching?

2. What do you find helpful or satisfying about behaviorist theory of learning? Does this seem to you to be the way you have learned things? Can you give examples either pro or con? How do you think this theory might be useful to you in your teaching?

3. In small groups or in a full class group, work out one or more well-stated behavioral objectives. Check to be sure each one specifies in precise terms 1) what the learner will be able to do, and 2) the criterion for minimum acceptable performance. (See Robert F. Mager, **Preparing Instructional Objectives**, Belmont, CA. Fearon, 1962.) Next, decide upon teaching strategies to accomplish the objective. Finally, discuss the result. Is your plan a satisfying lesson? What do you think about building a total Christian education program by this procedure?

4. What do you think about the needs-reduction theory of learning? Does this seem to be the way you have learned anything? Can you give an example? Do you think this theory might be useful to you in your teaching? How?

5. Do you think Maslow's list of the order of psychological development gives you any insights into primary children? Can this make you a better teacher? How?

6. Can you recall from childhood the effect that any particular story had on you? What do you remember about it? What insights does this give that you would like to carry over into your teaching? (Remember, memories of childhood can be distorted. See Chapter 4.)

Projects

1. Use a concordance and gather several verses about heart and mind as they relate to learning. What do these verses seem to tell you? Bring your conclusions or your questions to share with your study group.

2. Collect from published lessons or from teachers a list of

behavioral objectives. Analyze these to see if they are true behavioral objectives. That is, do they contain the specifics mentioned in discussion item 2?

3. Find a published lesson that claims to start with a need. Determine whether the need is a psychological one from Maslow's list or some other kind of need. Analyze what the lesson does with it. Does it truly reduce the need in the learners? Does it use the need as motivation to learn? Does it use the need to arouse interest or catch attention at the beginning of the lesson? Or does it use the need in some other way?

4. Conduct an interview with one or more primary children to try to determine their understanding of "family" or "promise" or another, concept of your choice.

Observation

Make arrangements to visit a primary class at a time when the children will be talking. See if you can find any remarks or incidents that give you hints about what a child's mental developmental level may be.

CHAPTER 3: BIBLE LEARNING

Discussion

1. What do you think about teaching primary children of sin, evil, and God's judgment? Try to justify your position from Scripture, and also from personal experience and common sense.

2. What do you think a child needs to know in order to be saved? What particular vocabulary would you use in leading a child to Christ? Why?

3. Can you remember what you thought about sin or salvation when you were a primary? If you were saved as a primary, what do you remember about your understanding of things at that time? Does this give you any help for teaching children? (Your memories, while helpful, may have changed over the years. See Chapter 4.)

Projects

1. Listen to several primary children read the Bible to you. Assess for each child what reading level the selection is on, as far as word recognition is concerned. Here are three levels and the percentage of words a child reads correctly.

    1) Independent Level: 99-100%

    2) Instructional Level: 90-95

    3) Frustration Level: Below 90

(A fuller inventory of a child's reading would include, also, a check on the meaning of the words and comprehension of the passage—both literal and inferential. So be cautioned not to make too much of the one score you obtain.)

2. In a similar way, test the children on Bible reading materials designed for their own grade levels.

3. Examine one or more published primary curriculums and try to determine what doctrines are taught in it.

4. Choose one or more of the doctrines mentioned in this chapter and interview several primary children concerning it. Try to determine what the children seem to understand about it. Do you find some children on a concrete level as Jenny in Chapter 2? And do you find some children beyond this? Explain the difference.

Observation

1. Observe in one or more public school primary reading classes. Jot down any ideas you feel will be helpful for teaching reading in Bible classes. Share your observations with your study group.

2. Observe a primary class where a doctrinal lesson is being taught. Watch the children closely for signs of understanding. Do their questions or comments tell you anything? Does their attention or lack of it tell you anything? What else can you learn from this observation?

CHAPTER 4: MEMORIZING AND REMEMBERING

Discussion

1. What do you remember about Scripture memorizing from your own childhood? What worked best? What didn't work so well? What features of this do you want to carry over into your own teaching? What would you like to do differently?

2. Have you had an experience of going back to some childhood location? Was it as you expected to find it, or not? Try to explain how your memory worked in this case.

3. When you are memorizing Scripture do you think of it mostly in images or mostly in its verbal meaning? Take a count in your class to see how many prefer each type of coding. How many think they use both types equally?

Projects

1. Here are Carnegie's memory pegs from 1 to 10. 1—run, 2—zoo, 3—tree, 4—door, 5—beehive, 6—sick, 7—Heaven, 8—gate, 9—wine, 10—den. You and your classmates spend several days memorizing them well. Take time enough to set them in your long-term memory. Then someday in class together use them to help you memorize one or both of these Sciptures with lists: Philippians 4:8; Galatians 5:22, 23. Share your various reactions to this system of memorizing.

2. Choose a short Scripture. Discuss together some images (meaningful ones) that can help in remembering it. Discuss, also, some semantic meanings (the order, the interrelationships of parts, clarified meanings of difficult phrases, etc.). Then everyone memorize the Scripture. Share your various reactions to the imagery or the semantic coding, and how they helped in memorizing.

3. Choose a Scripture passage appropriate for primary children to learn, and plan how you would teach it to a class group. Show how your plan makes use of coding (figural, semantic) and of time (mental rehearsal, repetition, spaced practice).

Observation

Arrange for two primary children to memorize a verse together. This is done with a pair so you can hear what's going on. Don't offer them help in how to do it, but offer a reward if you wish. Observe their memorizing. What use do you see of coding, repetition, and other aspects you know about memorizing? How could you help them become better memorizers?

CHAPTER 5: CURRICULUM

Discussion
1. What do you value? If you were on a curriculum committee just beginning from scratch, what would you suggest be included in the statement of purpose?

Projects
1. For one or more published curriculums (primary level) see if you can find out what organizing principle—sequence—was used as it was developed originally.

2. For the same curriculums try to determine the basic values it grew out of. Can you find evidence that it sticks closely to its stated or implied values? Do you find indications that at times it does not?

3. For the same curriculums, examine some lessons—about half of the lessons in one book and half in another. Would you say a curriculum uses mostly the psychological approach in its lessons, dwelling largely on needs and satisfying them? Or would you say it uses mostly the God-to-man approach of teaching God's revelation in a systematic and meaningful way?

Note: To do these projects you will have to read and think deeper than just scanning lesson objectives or some other quick method. Published curriculums are written for the teacher and not for the curriculum analyst, so you will not always find these things written out clearly for you. Also, for most curriculums you will find various mixes of the things you are looking for. You need to read far enough that you have a good feel for what a curriculum will do for primary children.

Observation
Arrange to read a particular primary lesson before you observe it. As you observe, have in your hand a copy of the teacher manual, or at least a set of notes you made as you read the lesson. Notice how closely the teacher sticks to the prepared lesson, and how much she deviates

from it. What did she add? What did she change? What did she leave out? Can you see reasons for these changes? In your opinion did they help the lesson or hurt it?

CHAPTER 6: TEACHING WITH STORIES

Discussion

1. Have you read or heard that you should not read to the children in Sunday school? What reasons were given for this advice? Do you think the advice was intended for stories as well as "sermonettes" or "lessons"? Do you think it **should** apply to stories as well as other things? Why or why not?

2. As a class group select a Bible story to use with children. Plan any preteaching you think should be done. Plan a listening task for the children. Decide how the story should be presented (reading, telling, visuals or not, what visuals). Plan one or more follow-up activities to strengthen the learning.

Projects

1. As an individual do the project described in discussion item 2.

2. Examine two primary curriculums and compare the use of stories in them. What similarities do you find? What differences?

3. From a public library obtain one or more children's books on the topic of death. Read them and give your opinion about the use of these books in Christian families or schools.

4. Find a good story. Practice it and read it to a group of children or to your teachers' study group. If your study group reads stories to each other, the group can follow up by listing ideas for being good story readers.

5. Do a project similar to 4, above, but tell a story instead of reading it.

Observations

1. Observe in a public library story hour. Notice whether the teacher reads some of the stories to the children. Jot down any ideas you get that will help you in presenting stories to children. (In a library you may be seeing a professional or a volunteer, and the quality of the story hours can vary.)

2. Arrange with a public school to observe in a primary story time.

Does the teacher read stories? Do the children listen? Do you think they enjoyed this part of their day?

CHAPTER 7:
TEACHING WITH ART

Discussion

1. Can you remember any incident from your own childhood when a teacher either encouraged you in art or discouraged you? You might share this memory if you think it will help others in your group know better how to help young children.

2. Do you think art or handwork is important enough to be included in every lesson? Why? Do you think it should only be used occasionally? Why?

3. What do you see as the best use(s) for art in a Christian education program?

4. Choose a Bible story and suggest what might be good art or drawing activities to help teach it.

Projects

1. Interview one or more art teachers to obtain their views on children's self-taught art, colorbook activities, copying drawings, and other areas of children's art that interest you or the teachers. Share your findings with your study group.

2. Obtain drawings from primary children of varied ages. On the basis of the drawings themselves, separate them into three piles: 1) less advanced, 2) middle or unable to decide, and 3) most advanced. Study piles 1 and 3. What differences do you see? What are some of the things children seem to learn as they progress from your classification 1 to classification 3?

Observation

1. Observe some children drawing things they are much interested in. Jot down notes of what they say and do as they work.

CHAPTER 8:
TEACHING WITH
ACTIVITIES

Discussion

1. Have you been in a class recently which used an activity? How valuable do you think it was? What kinds of activities help you most? Are there any kinds which seem a waste of your time?

2. Have you taught recently with an activity? How helpful do you think it was? Have you ever tried an activity which you felt was not very valuable?

3. Do you think there should be differences between children and adults in the amount of activity used in teaching? What?

Project

Select a Bible story for teaching primaries. Plan a story activity and vocabulary activity to go with it.

Observation

1. Arrange to observe in a primary class that uses activities. As you watch the children, do you get indications of what they are learning? How? Do you see specific ways an activity helps one or more children learn something? What is your opinion of the particular activities you observed?

CHAPTER 9:
THE TEACHER

Discussion

1. Can you think of something or someone who encouraged or helped you in your teaching? Do you have anything encouraging or helpful to pass along to others in your study group?

2. Can you think of a classroom incident where you felt successful in your teaching? Try to think, also, of a time when you learned something meaningful while you were a student in a class. As your group shares these items, compile a list of the teaching methods that were used on these occasions. What do you learn from the list?

3. Consider the activity method of teaching. Do you think it is the best way to teach? Why or why not? What are some things that can be taught well by this method? What kinds of pupils might be taught well by this method? Name a situation where another method might be better. (Use your commonsense teaching knowledge to answer these questions.)

4. Consider another method you or someone in your study group is interested in. Discuss it, using the starter questions in item 3.

Projects

1. Carry out the four-step exercise suggested in this chapter.

2. Pretend that the superintendent has said he must move one child from your class to another. Which child would you send? Next, imagine that you could keep one child for another year (without him feeling he has been held back). Which child would you choose to keep? Analyze why you made these choices. What does this tell you about your teaching relationship to these and to your other children?

3. Imagine that the parents will be talking to you after a Sunday school program. Which child would you feel least prepared to talk about? Plan a strategy to rectify this.

Observation

This is a reverse observation task. Invite a friend to observe as you teach. Give your friend the specific task of noticing whether there are differences in the way you treat the various children. Do you call on some more than others? Do you wait more patiently for some to answer? Do you rephrase your question for some and give them a second opportunity to answer, while with others you simply call on another child if the first misses a question? Does your tone of voice betray different attitudes toward different children?

See what you can learn from your friend's observation. An alternate way to do this task is to run a tape recorder during your class session. Try analyzing it yourself, or perhaps with a friend or advisor.

Index